Painting More Animals on Rocks

LIN WELLFORD

NORTH LIGHT BOOKS

CINCINNATI, OHIO

ABOUT THE AUTHOR

Lin Wellford readily acknowledges her good fortune in receiving early encouragement that fostered her interest in art. Pen-and-ink sketches and watercolor landscapes played a part in her evolution as an artist, as did three years' study of advertising design at the University of Florida. Moving to the Arkansas Ozarks opened the door to her career as a "rock artist" and has provided an ongoing source of inspiration. As with her previous books, *The Art of Painting Animals on Rocks* and *Painting Houses, Cottages and Towns on Rocks*, she hopes this book will inspire others to see the creative possibilities in rocks and perhaps discover hidden talents within themselves. Also watch for her upcoming book, *Painting Flowers on Rocks*.

Wellford lives in Green Forest, Arkansas, with her husband, Klaus. They are the parents of three daughters.

Painting More Animals on Rocks. Copyright © 1998 by Lin Wellford. Manufactured in China. All rights reserved. No part of this book may be reproduced in any form or by any electronic or mechanical means including information storage and retrieval systems without permission in writing from the publisher, except by a reviewer, who may quote brief passages in a review. Published by North Light Books, an imprint of F&W Publications, Inc., 4700 East Galbraith Road, Cincinnati, Ohio 45236. (800) 289-0963. First edition.

Other fine North Light Books are available from your local bookstore, art supply store or direct from the publisher.

06 05 04 03   11 10 9 8

Library of Congress Cataloging-in-Publication Data

Wellford, Lin.
    Painting more animals on rocks / by Lin Wellford.
        p. cm.
    Includes index.
    ISBN 0-89134-800-X (alk. paper)
    1. Stone painting. 2. Acrylic painting. 3. Animals in art. I. Title.
TT370.W464 1998
751.4′26—dc21   97-17887
                                                                      CIP

Edited by Jennifer Long
Production edited by Jennifer Lepore and Katie Carroll
Interior designed by Julie Martin
Cover designed by Kathleen DeZarn

DEDICATION

For Robin Greeson and Fayrene
Farmer with love and
appreciation. My thanks also to
David Lewis at North Light Books
for seeing the possibilities.

Table *of* Contents

Painting More Animals on Rocks

Introduction

Ever since North Light Books published my first volume of rock painting projects, *The Art of Painting Animals on Rocks*, I've been thrilled by the number of people who've joined the ranks of avid rock painters. Like me, they've discovered that there is something almost magical about transforming plain old rocks into arresting works of art. It's even more exciting to hear from people who never thought of themselves as artistic, but, with a little guidance and patience, have realized they are capable of creating wonderful things.

I believe everyone is born with the seeds of artistic ability, but not everyone is blessed with a nurturing environment where those seeds can germinate. Some people are told as children that they have no talent. This withers their confidence and with it their interest in making art.

Rock painting is an especially good avenue for rediscovering those dormant abilities. Rocks and stones come with clearly defined shapes, so it's easier to make choices about what and where to paint. And since stones are three dimensional, a beginning painter is not confronted with the perplexing task of making a flat surface look like it's not. Best of all, rocks are a free and plentiful resource, so you can experiment without worrying about "wasting" anything of value. More experienced painters appreciate the fact that their finished artwork does not require expensive matting and framing.

Yet another big rock painting plus is that hunting for good rocks to paint is as much fun as actually painting them. It's a great excuse to spend time outdoors and can turn into an exciting adventure for the whole family.

Rock painting is also an ideal, low cost recreation for groups. Kids of all ages love to paint on rocks in classroom settings or as summer camp projects. Senior citizens and hobby groups have incorporated rock painting into their schedules, too.

I hope that looking through the pages of this book will intrigue, excite and, most of all, inspire you to pick up a paintbrush and reclaim the artist within. Happy painting!

WHERE TO LOOK FOR ROCKS

The projects in this book use a variety of rock sizes and shapes, from pebbles to the biggest rock you care to pick up and stagger home with. I like to use rocks with corners and edges that have been smoothed and rounded by the action of ocean tides or by being tumbled along riverbeds. Such rocks are common throughout large portions of this country and around the world, but not all rivers have enough current to produce rounded rocks, so you may need to ask around to find a good source in your area. Hunters and fishermen can often direct you to promising sites.

Even in Florida and along the Gulf Coast where shells, not rocks, are washed ashore, with a little effort you can still find good rocks to paint. Some garden centers keep larger river rocks on hand for landscaping projects, or, for a few dollars, you can purchase a fifty-pound bag of assorted pebbles and smaller rocks. I did this and found many suitable rocks for frogs, mice and penguins among the contents. Near my hometown of Sarasota, Florida, I located a rock yard that had an acre or more of stones divided by type and size. They sold them mostly to contractors for facing fireplaces and other building projects, but they were willing to sell me the ones I selected for fifty cents each, still cheap compared to most art supplies.

Another solution if you live in a rockless area is to fill up your trunk next time you're traveling, but be sure to ask any nearby landowner if it's okay to take a few rocks. I've never had anyone turn me down, but they appreciate being asked. And, of course, avoid rock collecting in state or national parks.

The author, her husband and two of her daughters on a family rock hunt.

Bought by the bag from a landscaper, these smaller rocks are perfect for tiny critters.

Painting More Animals on Rocks

SUPPLIES
Paints

Besides rocks, you will need a few bottles of liquid acrylic paint, available at any art supply or craft shop and in many large discount stores. You can complete nearly every project in this book using the same handful of colors: black, white, red, Burnt Sienna and Yellow Ochre (Antique Gold or Harvest Gold can be substituted for Yellow Ochre in all of these projects). Blue, bright green, bright yellow, Metallic Gold and Nutmeg Brown are used to complete one or two more projects.

Brushes

You also need at least one good quality liner brush. I've used many different kinds, but keep going back to Lowe-Cornell's Script Liner in a size 0 or 1. These brushes are ideal for the delicate fur lines that add so much to the overall appearance of rock animals. An assortment of other inexpensive brushes in various sizes and shapes will come in handy, as will any old, worn out brushes you may have, especially ones with separated bristles.

If you're going to buy brushes, in addition to a liner brush, get a medium-size square brush ½" to ¾" (12 to 19mm) wide and a couple of tapered brushes in sizes that fall between the square brush and the liner. A small, short-bristled detail brush is also useful.

Other Supplies

I recommend Sharpies or other fine-lined but sturdy markers for sketching over layout lines and signing your finished work. Keep a good supply of sharpened pencils ready, too, and some chalk or white-lead pencils. For a few projects, a straightedge will come in handy. You will need scissors, scrap leather or fabric, and household glue or wood filler to make the tails of two of the animals. And save your old newspapers: Newsprint provides the perfect work surface.

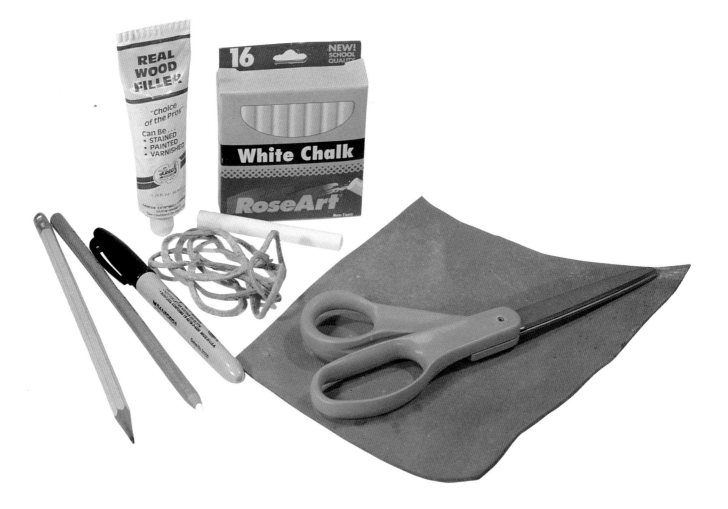

Painting More Animals on Rocks

HELPFUL HINTS

To make them easier to paint, I have simplified some of the details for my animal projects. You may want to start collecting photographs and clippings of these animals to help you achieve even more realistic detail, or to discover other poses and expressions you can adapt to the pieces you paint.

This book offers guidelines and suggestions to help you achieve initial results of which you can be proud. As you continue to paint, your own unique style will begin to assert itself. This is perfectly natural. Like handwriting, everyone has their own distinct way of painting. You should seek to develop your personal style, not suppress it.

Finally, and perhaps most importantly, enjoy the process. Be patient with yourself and with your developing skills. It may be frustrating not to get the results you hoped for at first, but (trust me on this) my first animals did not look like the ones I paint now. With any luck, the way I paint five years down the line will be very different from what I'm able to do now. It is part of the creative growth and development we are all capable of experiencing.

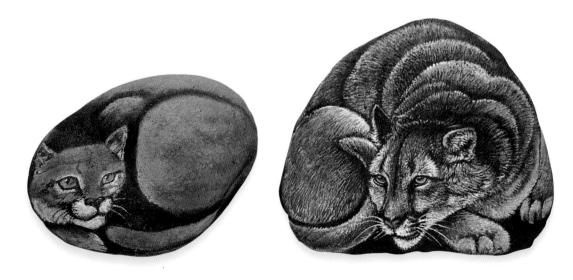

I painted the cougar on the left in 1982 and the one on the right in 1996. With a little practice anyone can improve their painting skills. Just think what you'll be painting a year from now!

Painting More Animals on Rocks

How to Paint a
Frog

These colorful little amphibians are a popular collectible in a variety of mediums: ceramic, glass, metal, even carved stone. Painting frogs on rocks is an easy and fun way to add to such a collection (or to start a new one).

Frogs and their toad cousins come in an array of patterns and sizes. Just thumbing through a book on reptiles will give you some idea of their mind boggling variety.

For this project, I chose the leopard, or spotted, frog. All frogs and toads can be painted on a number of commonly found stone shapes, ranging from simple ovals to gently contoured diamonds or teardrop shapes. The oval rock I've selected is 3″ to 4″ (7.6cm to 10.2cm) long. You may prefer to do a larger or smaller version.

What You'll Need
• acrylic paints in bright green, bright yellow, white, black, dark brown and metallic gold
• pencil
• assorted brushes

This selection of "froggy" rocks represents a few of the many options you have when searching for just the right stone to paint.

An oval rock like this one is a common shape and a good choice.

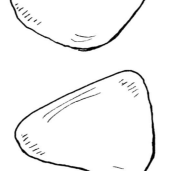

Here are some of the more desirable shapes to look for.

1 Base Coat

Mix bright green and bright yellow paint together to get a light green shade. Use a round or square brush to cover the top and sides of your rock, leaving only the very bottom surface unpainted. (Make sure your rock is clean before you paint it.) Let dry.

Next, paint the bottom surface white up to the edges of your green paint. Curve the white up slightly at the neck on both sides to define the shape of the frog's head. When the paint has dried, you're ready to lay out the features.

Cover the top and sides with a coat of green paint. You may need more than one coat for solid coverage.

Paint the underside of the rock white.

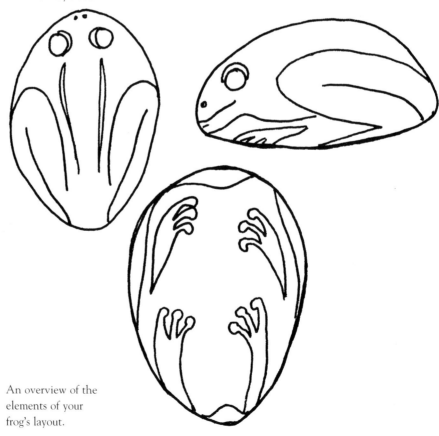

An overview of the elements of your frog's layout.

Painting More Animals on Rocks

2 Layout

Use a sharpened pencil to sketch in the front and back feet on the bottom of your rock. Place tiny balls at the end of each toe. Fill in the feet with the same light green color, using a script liner or other detail brush. Create a slightly pointy bump to help define your frog's tail end. Allow these areas to dry.

Sketch in the feet first. Note the length of the toes and their ball-like ends.

Use a short, narrow brush to paint the front and back feet, keeping them long and narrow.

This little bump suggests a tail end.

Now use your pencil to sketch in the doubled up back legs, eyes, mouth and nostrils. Make sure the eyes are level to avoid a cockeyed look.

Imagine long frog legs doubled up neatly along the creature's sides.

Sketch in the facial features. Widely spaced eyes and a broad mouth are characteristic of all frogs.

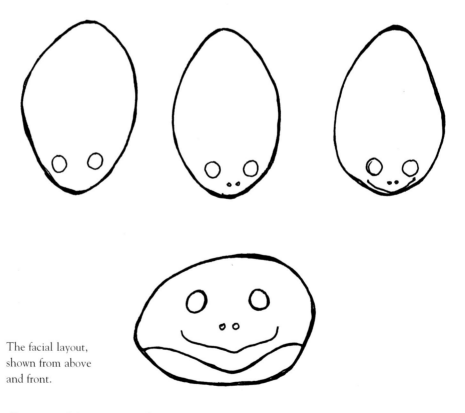

The facial layout, shown from above and front.

Painting More Animals on Rocks

3 Outlines

Dip your script liner brush into black paint and narrowly outline the feet and toes. Also go over the guidelines you just sketched in.

Switch to white paint and add highlights. Begin by outlining a half circle beneath each eye. Extend this narrow line along the back, bowing it out slightly before tapering it off near the rear end. Use white to highlight along the lower line of the two folded back legs. Emphasize the shape of the mouth by making a white line above and below it.

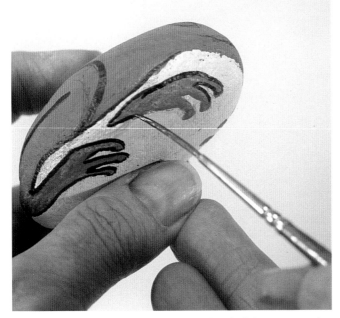

Carefully outline all the way around the sketched features to make them stand out.

White lines along the back add to the frog's streamlined look. Note how these lines extend to encircle the bottom half of each eye.

Place a white streak along the curve of the lower portion of the leg. White outlines on both sides of the mouth line make it stand out.

4 Markings

Use brown paint and a slightly larger brush to create a series of tandem oval-shaped markings along the frog's back, inside the curving white lines. Complete the back markings with a few smaller, irregular spots outside the white lines just above where the legs curve out from the rear. Finally, add pointed top markings that begin along the center curved line of the legs.

Use your liner brush to create eyelids above either eye. Extend this line from the front center edge of each eye, angling toward the nostrils. While these lines are wet, soften them by smudging the paint lightly with your fingertip. Still using brown paint, make a shading line of brown along the outside edge of both white lines on the back.

Add large gold centers to all the brown spots along your frog's back and legs. Fill in the eye circles with metallic gold as well.

Dark brown spots in graduating sizes are an important element of this frog's design. For added emphasis, use the same brown to shadow the white lines. Add a half circle eyelid line above each eye and angle this line out to meet the nostrils.

Add metallic gold centers to the brown spots, leaving dark outlines showing. Gold eyes lend a realistic shimmer.

Pattern for spots on back and legs.

5 Finishing Touches

Use a small, short bristled brush and additional yellow paint to mix a noticeably brighter shade of green than that used for the frog's body. Keep your brush rather dry and scrub this bright yellow-green along the top edge of both legs (being careful not to cover up any lines or spots). Brighten the skin tone along the spine and on the sides just below the white lines with the same "scrubby" strokes.

Finally, use your script liner to place a horizontal black iris in the center of both eyes. Allow it to dry, then use a dab of white to add a gleam at the same place on both eyes.

Now look over your frog carefully to make sure all surfaces are painted and all lines are clear. Sign your work on the tummy with a Sharpie or other fine-tipped marker. A light coating of clear enamel, either sprayed or brushed on, will bring out the colors more vividly and protect the finish.

Blending lighter skin tones along the top edges of the legs and along the back gives your piece added dimension.

Paint horizontal black irises. Tiny white dots make the eyes appear wet.

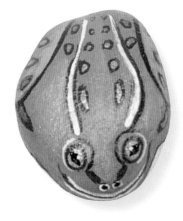

A family of leopard frogs, ready to leap.

More Ideas . . .

Flat, circular stones painted as lily pads make attractive bases for displaying your frogs, and can also be incorporated into table top water gardens.

Here's how to paint a lily pad rock.

Frogs make perfect companions for house plants. Try putting together an easy care terrarium—just add water and enjoy!

Painting More Animals on Rocks

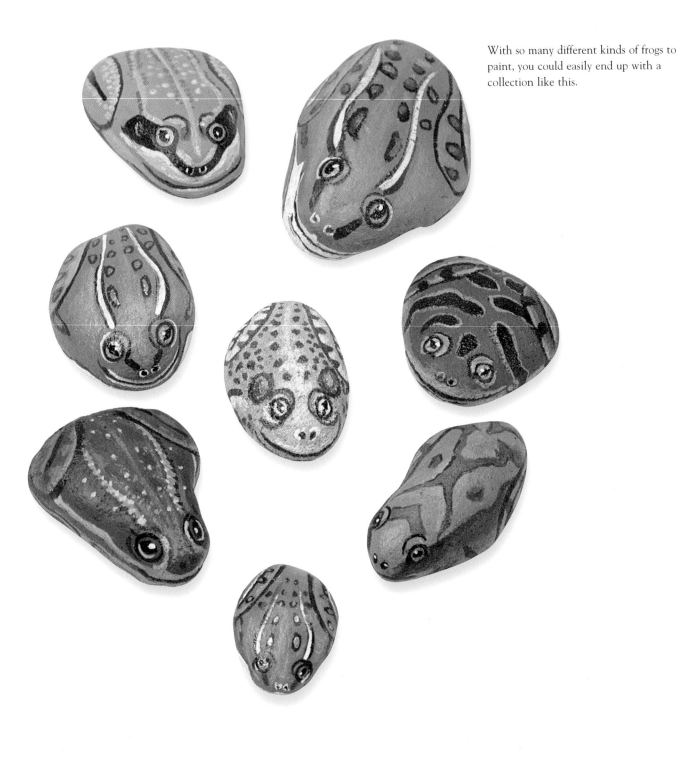

With so many different kinds of frogs to paint, you could easily end up with a collection like this.

Painting More Animals on Rocks

How to Paint a
Field Mouse

A furry gray field mouse with bright eyes and a pink tail makes a great subject for beginning rock painters. Rock mice can also be painted in white or subtle shades of brown.

As with the frogs in the previous project, look for rocks that are basically oval, either short and plump or more elongated. The best ones will also have one tapered or pointed end to serve as the nose. They can be up to 4″ or 5″ (10.2cm or 12.7cm) long (any bigger and they look more like rats), or much smaller if you want to make a baby mouse. Remember, though, that painting very small details can be more difficult. I advise trying a larger size mouse first. For the tails, rawhide lacing is available at most large craft stores, or you can cut a tail from a thin strip of felt.

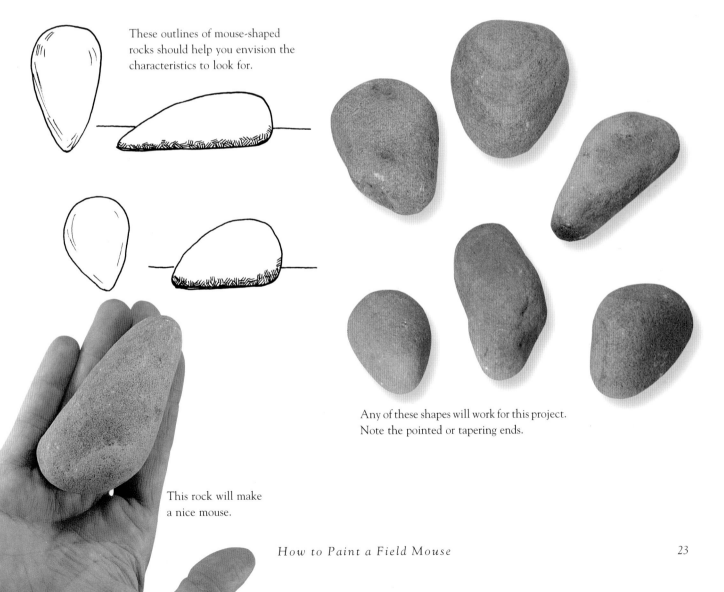

These outlines of mouse-shaped rocks should help you envision the characteristics to look for.

Any of these shapes will work for this project. Note the pointed or tapering ends.

This rock will make a nice mouse.

1 Base Coat

Make sure the rock you've chosen is scrubbed clean before you begin painting. Mix together roughly equal parts of black and white paint to get a medium shade of gray. Use a large brush to quickly cover the top and sides of the rock, leaving a narrow strip around the bottom edge unpainted. When the paint is dry, switch to a clean brush and use white paint to cover the entire bottom of the rock and the unpainted strip around the sides.

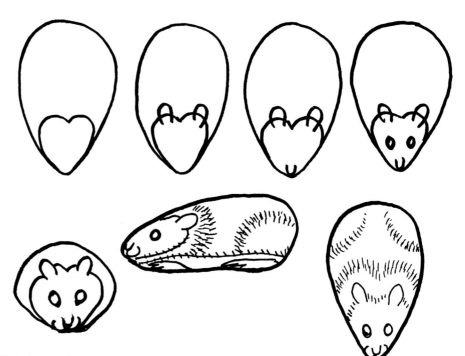

Basic layout of mouse features as seen from several angles.

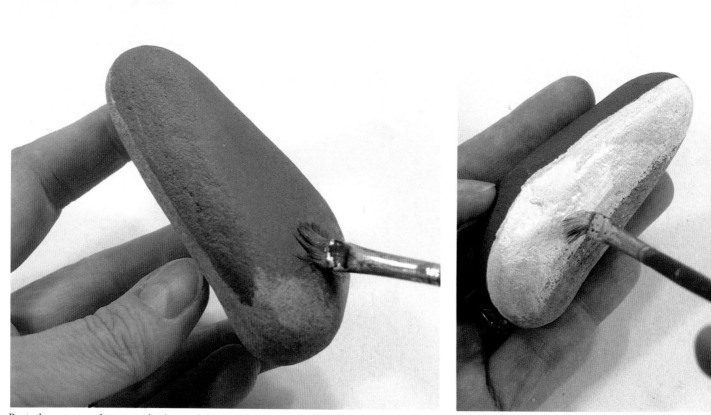

Begin by painting the top and sides a solid gray, leaving an unpainted edge along the base.

Paint the entire bottom and lower edge of the sides white.

Painting More Animals on Rocks

2 Layout

Wait until the base coat is dry before using a pencil to sketch in the features. Begin by outlining the head in an elongated heart shape. Place small round or oval ears along the top curves of the head. Tuck a small, **U**-shaped nose at the pointed tip of your heart shape. Two round eyes should be spaced at least one eye-width apart and situated midway between the nose and the ears. Indicate semicircle muzzle shapes on either side of the nose.

Next, turn your mouse over and sketch the long, narrow front and rear feet. Your mouse will look cuter if you position the feet so that they are partially visible from the sides.

3 Fur

With black paint and a liner or other detail brush, outline the ears, eyes, nose and muzzle lines to make them stand out clearly. Go around the entire head with a series of tiny fur lines. Then use more closely spaced, dense strokes to create the curves of shoulders and the round shapes of the haunches. Once these basic contours are in place, make more short, tapering strokes along the back and sides, overlapping and crisscrossing these delicate strokes in a random fashion to simulate fur, as shown in the directional guide on the next page. Turn your rock as needed to facilitate the application of brushstrokes. Add even shorter, more delicate splinter-type strokes to the forehead and up along the center of the muzzle from just above the nose. Encircle the area below each eye with tiny black fur lines, too. While you have black on your brush, this is a good time to fill in the eye circles, giving your mouse its bright, beady-looking eyes.

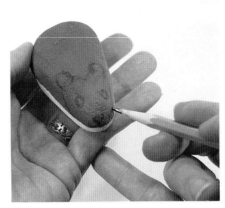

Sketch in your mouse's face. Keep the eyes widely spaced and set them midway between the top of the head and the tip of the nose.

Place the front and rear feet so they show along the sides of the rock.

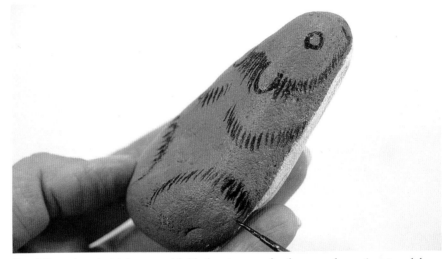

Carefully outline facial features with black paint to make them stand out. A series of short, tapering lines delineate body contours while beginning to build up a fuzzy, furry texture.

Varying the length and direction of your strokes as you add layers of detail will contribute to the realistic look of your mouse.

How to Paint a Field Mouse

4 Pink Areas

Now clean your brush and mix a small amount of red into a larger amount of white paint to get a soft pink shade. Use pink to color the sketched-in front and back feet. Also use pink to fill in the **U**-shaped nose and the centers of the ears.

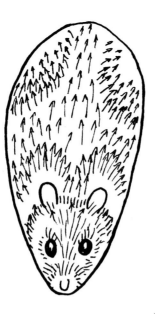

Start detailing the face just above the nose and work your way up, allowing the delicate fur lines to splay out as the head widens. Scatter tiny fur lines into the area between the muzzle and eye, too. These sketches show the direction that mouse fur naturally grows.

Paint the front and rear feet pink. Three or four narrow toes are all you need.

Fill in the **U**-shape of the nose and the centers of the ears.

Detail of eyelash strokes. These are important because they frame the eyes.

Painting More Animals on Rocks

5 Finishing Touches

Still using a liner or detail brush, change to white paint and add the details that will bring your little mouse to life. First, highlight the tops of each eye with a series of eyelash-like strokes, starting with an outline from the front that sweeps around to the back as shown. Along the bottom of the eye, fan out another row of much shorter lash lines. Then, just above the edge of the head shape, overlap a series of light fur strokes outward, tapering them off before they completely cover the black fur lines. Do the same across the top of the head along the base of and between the ears. Paint a half circle of very small strokes, like prickles, around either side of the muzzle.

Now look for any plain gray area that needs the softening effect of light colored fur strokes, always remembering to angle them away from the head. Emphasize the shoulder and haunch contours in particular, highlighting the darker fur lines with a matching series of white ones. Scatter a few thin fur lines randomly over the back and sides. Soften the white strip along the bottom by stroking some paler fur lines down from the gray areas above.

With the tip of your brush, place a white dot in each eye to give it a sparkle. Experiment on scrap paper to insure the paint is not too thick or thin before adding several sweeping whiskers from each side of the muzzle.

Go around the bottom of the feet with a thin outline of Burnt Sienna to clearly define them. Now look your mouse over to see if there are any other areas that require more detail or definition. If you're satisfied, use a bit of household glue or wood filler to secure the tail to the bottom of the rock at the rear edge. A light coating of spray-on clear acrylic will protect the finish and enrich the hues of your paint.

White brushstrokes accentuate the contours and add texture. Cluster white fur lines along curves to suggest highlighting.

White dots lend a bright sparkle to the eyes. Test your paint consistency before sweeping narrow whiskers out from either side of the muzzle.

Attach a short tail to the bottom of the rock, close to the rear edge.

More Ideas . . .

Using the same basic steps, you can create a lively assortment of mice in many sizes and colors. A mama mouse and several little mouslings make a particularly appealing group. Or try painting a wedge-shaped rock to resemble cheese and pose your mouse with it.

These mice show the different color variations possible.

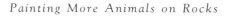

Painting More Animals on Rocks

A rock painted to look like a wedge of Swiss cheese makes a playful prop for your mouse rock.

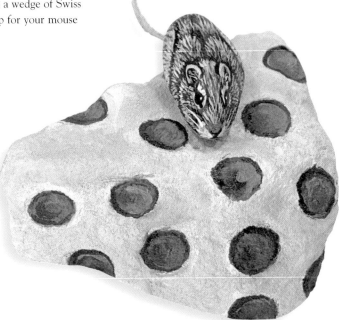

A tiny mouse makes a perfect "pocket pet."

Painting More Animals on Rocks

How to Paint a
Penguin

Perky penguins make a unique subject for rock painting, and their design is so simple that even beginning artists will enjoy creating them. For this project choose rocks that "sit up," in shapes ranging from narrow tombstones to plump pears, or even small, gently rounded rockets. The stone you select should be taller than it is wide, and while it can look somewhat asymmetrical, it should stand sturdily on its base.

Penguins can be just about any size, from larger-than-life to smaller than your pinky finger. For this project I found a rock that has two attractive features: It is fairly symmetrical and neatly pear shaped. Unfortunately, the base is a bit thin, making it prone to tipping. To correct this, I add a line of wood filler to one side of the base, molding it into place and securing it firmly before smoothing the surface.

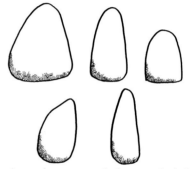

Outlines of penguin rock shapes to look for.

Any of these rocks are suitable for a penguin.

The addition of some wood filler corrects a tippy base.

This pear-shaped rock is a good choice. Smaller rocks may prove more challenging.

1 Layout

After your rock is scrubbed and dry and any additions to even out the base have cured, you are ready to begin your layout. Placement of the head will depend on how much your rock tapers, so select the design that most closely fits your particular rock shape. Since my rock has a pointy top, the head can be set fairly high. For more rounded, less pointed rocks, create a head that droops down as if resting against the bird's chest.

The shape of the head is a simple oval with a long narrow beak. Curve in the flipper-shaped wings as shown. On the back side, the bird's only marking is a large black diamond shape, with the top flowing up to serve as an extension of the neck while the bottom tapers neatly to a pointed tail. Before going on, look over your layout to see how it compares to my examples on the next page.

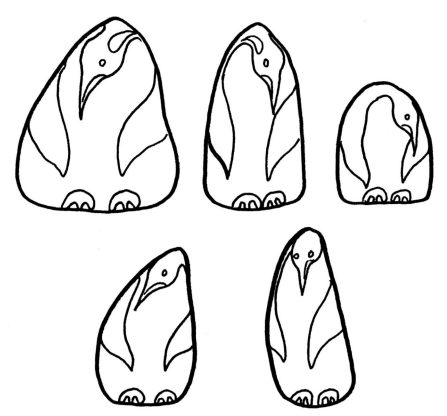

These sketches show how to adapt penguin features to different rock shapes.

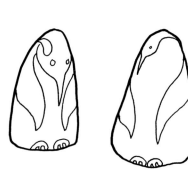

Two common mistakes are making the head too large, as on the left, or too small as shown on the right.

Begin by placing the head, then move on to sketch the wings as they curve in from either side.

Think of the back as a diamond, with the top end merging into the neck and the other end forming a pointed tail.

Painting More Animals on Rocks

2 Base Coat

Only two colors are needed to complete the base coat: black and white. Begin with white and a medium-sized brush. Cover the chest area, the areas surrounding the wings and around the head and beak. On the back side, paint only the area showing below the diamond shape and up under the rear edges of the wings. Allow your white paint to dry, then switch to black paint and use the same size brush to fill in all remaining areas, being careful to keep outside edges smooth. Use a narrow brush for the beak.

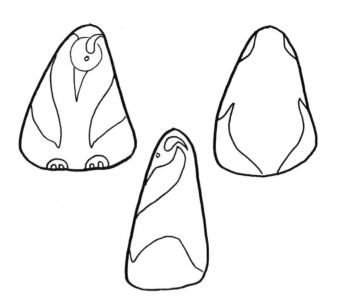

Views of the basic layout from several angles.

Paint in the white areas of the front and sides. If your rock is dark it may require more than one coat.

This rear view shows how simple the design is.

Allow your white paint to dry before you move to black. Note how carefully I worked to keep the black edges smooth.

3 Feet and Beak

Create black feet that peep out from the base of your penguin. Shape them like rounded lowercase **m**'s. Next, use a liner brush and a mixture of red and yellow, or premixed orange, to make a paisley-shaped marking on either side of the penguin's head, extending the tapered end back along the contour of the neck. With the same orange, add a narrow curve of color to the bottom edge of your penguin's beak. I've turned my penguin's head slightly to one side, but if yours is looking straight on, make the orange beak markings thinner and have them show on both sides.

Clean your brush and switch to bright yellow, adding an outline around the orange head markings to make them stand out. Moisten your brush tip to dilute your yellow paint slightly, then scribble color lightly onto the white area just below the curve of the head. Use your finger to gently smudge and soften this color so it blends into the surrounding area of the upper chest.

These stylized feet may barely show, but they're a nice touch.

Orange markings add an important visual element. Beak markings are nothing more than a thin crescent of color. Use a small detail brush or the tip of a liner brush for more control.

A thin yellow outline around the orange head markings increases their impact.

Add yellow paint to the area just below the neck and blend it downward with your finger, softening it to a sunny blush.

Painting More Animals on Rocks

4 Finishing Touches

The remaining brushwork will give your penguin added realism and texture. Use your script liner and mix equal parts of black and white paint to get a medium gray shade. Beginning at the back side of your penguin's head, make a row of very delicate, very short lines that taper back and away from the face. Add a second and third overlapping row of strokes, fanning them out and lengthening your strokes down into the upper back area before stopping. To highlight the wings, angle the same kinds of tiny strokes down along the upper and lower edges of the wings. Finish the back by adding more of the same fine lines along all outside edges.

Indicate the eye (or eyes) with a small circle of gray placed midway between the orange head marking and the orange beak marking.

Small highlighting strokes help define your penguin's contours while suggesting the texture of feathers. More delicate lines along the flipper-shaped wings give them extra substance.

Detail the back sides with the same kind of tiny strokes.

Define the eyes with simple gray circles. Because I have my penguin's head turned to the side, only one eye shows.

Use more of the medium gray paint to indicate shading in the center of your penguin just above the feet. This will help emphasize the shape of the legs on either side. Use feathery strokes in varied lengths, extending the longest ones upward until they extend beyond the level of the wing tips. Finally, with a relatively dry brush (a brush with very little paint) add one or two long, sketchy lines just inside and following along the contour of the head to give it shape. Now look your penguin over from every angle to make sure you've defined and detailed wherever needed. A light spray of polyurethane will bring out the richness of your colors and protect the finish.

Feathery shadows between the legs create the illusion of contour.

A highlighting line following the shape of the head makes it appear rounder.

Finished penguin.

Painting More Animals on Rocks

More Ideas . . .

Penguins are particularly attractive in small groupings. You may also want to try a parent and chick combination, which makes a delightful gift or eye-catching conversation piece on a desktop. Another fun idea is to create a snow-covered scene to set off your penguin, using white rocks to form a base.

This flock of penguins illustrates how different poses and different species make for a lot of possibilities.

Painting More Animals on Rocks

How to Paint a
Skunk

With their bold black and white coloring and a full, feathery tail unfurled overhead, skunks make striking subjects for rock painting. And with no distinctive aroma to worry about, stone skunks positively invite attention and admiration.

While it's sometimes possible to find a rock with both a rounded, arching back, and a tapering, somewhat blunt end to serve as a head, it's much easier to come by plain, half-round rocks. On such a rock the head can be set so that the skunk is looking back over its body. The base of the rock should be flat.

While these assorted rocks differ in many ways, all have the arched top required to accommodate a skunk's raised tail.

What You'll Need

- acrylic paints in black, white, Burnt Sienna and red
- chalk or white-lead pencil
- assorted brushes

This flat-bottomed, half-round rock is just what I was looking for.

Some basic layouts with possible variations.

39

1 Base Coat

Make sure the surface is clean and dry before using a wide brush to cover the entire rock with black paint. Allow this base coat to dry.

2 Layout

Select the best side for the head. If your rock's surface has any flaws, choose the smoother side. Use a piece of chalk or a white-lead pencil to sketch in the basic features. Place the head low enough so there will be lots of room for the tail. Proportionally, the head should take about one-third of the width across the front surface of your rock. Its shape is somewhat triangular, with a slight upward tilt to the tip of the nose. Add a rounded cap to the top third of the triangle, the hairline slanting downward as shown. Set the eye circle midway between the nose and the base of the cap. Place a small round ear even with the eye, as far from the eye as the eye is from the nose.

Next, sketch in the side stripe. Begin with a narrow line curving up and out from the top of the skunk's head. Allow this streak to dip down as it travels across the front surface, widening as it goes, until you reach the curved end of the rock. At that point, extend the bottom line around the curve, angling it up to taper into the upper line.

Lay out the tail by stroking in a series of curving lines beginning at the base of the tail. Each stroke should get successively longer before curving out, creating a plume-like cascade of tendrils that follows the arch of the back, extending into the area just above the skunk's white cap. On the rear side, create a matching streak and duplicate the lines of the cascading tail. Keep the feet simple as shown, tucked along the base of the rock.

Paint the entire rock black. Chalk shows up well against the black base coat—and it's easy to wash it off and try again until you're happy with your layout.

Breaking the layout down into easy-to-follow steps demonstrates that there's nothing tricky about drawing this animal.

Painting More Animals on Rocks

3 White Areas

Using a large round or square brush and white paint, block in your white areas. An older brush with stiff bristles is ideal for stroking in a ragged edge that simulates individual fur lines. Add a duplicate streak of white on the rear side. Next, use your brush to scrub in the white cap that tops the skunk's head, angling your strokes upward to create the look of fur. Extend a small streak of white from the base of the cap, slanting across the forehead toward the nose.

Switch to a script liner to work on the tail. Begin near the base at the tail end, where the side stripes meet. Draw the individual fur lines upward before curving and tapering them off into the plain area above the side streak. Leave a dark strip between the tips of the tail fur and the side streak for contrast. Overlap some of these tail lines for a naturally random look. Still using your script liner, create the impression of fur by outlining the basic shape of the face and feet with tiny, prickle-type strokes. Fill in the inside area of each foot with more short lines. Go over the sketched outlines of the ear and eyes with white paint.

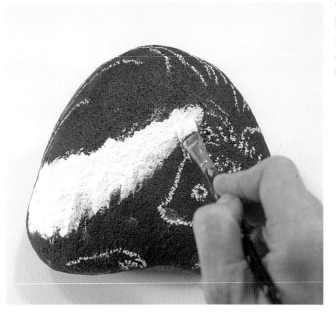

Use the end of your brush to create the ragged look of fur along the side streaks.

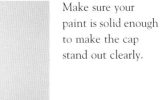

Make sure your paint is solid enough to make the cap stand out clearly.

Follow these simple steps to paint a perfect foot.

Your skunk's tail tendrils are a vital element. Vary the width of your strokes as well as the direction for added realism. Do one set to define the overall shape, then go back and add more layers of tendrils until you've created a substantial tail your skunk can be proud of.

4 Base Coat the Features

Mix a touch of red into a larger droplet of white to get a medium pink color. Use it to paint a small pink nose, and to fill in the center of the ear. Switch to Burnt Sienna and darken it to a deeper brown by adding a touch of black. Fill in the eye circle with this color. Now all your basic colors are in place.

5 Fur Details

To add more definition to your skunk, use black paint and your script liner. Begin along the top of your side streaks, stroking downward with a series of varied lines, some longer, some shorter, some closer together than others. Use the same fur lines to detail the bottom edge of the side streak. Next, go all around the top of the skunk's furry cap with very short, prickly strokes.

Mix up a small batch of gray paint next and begin to detail the black areas with fine gray fur lines. These gray strokes should stop well short of the

Fill in the nose and ears with pink to add a welcome touch of color.

bordering white areas, leaving dark edges for added contrast. Once you're satisfied with the amount of fur detailing, switch to black paint to reemphasize the individual toes on the skunk's feet. The white outlines around the eye

may also need some retouching for a cleaner look. At the same time, add a small black oval iris to the eye. You may want to shade the white outline around the ear to make it stand out.

Paint in a dark brown eye. Don't worry about the chalk outlines—they'll disappear under your wet paint.

These small fur lines help define the features and add realistic texture. Note how the heavy concentration of lines around the curve of the cap differentiates it from the tail behind it.

Painting More Animals on Rocks

This fur directional guide shows how to handle areas of detail.

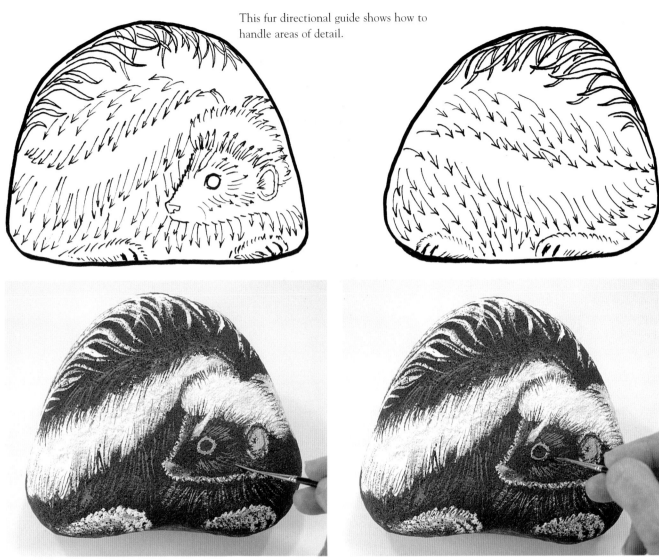

Gray fur lines will give the black areas of your animal a softer, more realistic appearance. Note how I used paler gray strokes to frame the bottom of the head.

Attention to small details will give your piece a more finished look. Use small black lines to define the foot fur and outline the eye circle. Paint a dark iris in the center of the eye.

Make sure you go over your chalk outlines with paint. (Both the ear outline and the shape of the head were still only chalked in.) For the ear, use a plain curved line, but switch to rows of tiny, splinter type strokes around the face.

How to Paint a Skunk

6 Finishing Touches

Carefully draw out several whiskers from either side of the muzzle using white paint. A small dot of white placed at the edge of the skunk's iris completes the piece. Looking over my skunk, however, I decided that a few contrasting strokes of Burnt Sienna along the bridge of the nose would add interest to the face. You may also use these touches of Burnt Sienna to outline the lower portions of some of the tail tendrils.

When you have completed your skunk, spray or brush the piece with polyurethane to heighten the colors and protect the paint.

Do test strokes to check paint consistency before stroking in the whiskers. A tiny dot of white adds life to the eye.

The addition of some touches of Burnt Sienna warms up the face and the base of the tail tendrils.

Painting More Animals on Rocks

More Ideas . . .

Since baby skunks are identical to adults except smaller, try creating a whole family and display them parading through your garden. Spotted skunks are yet another variation you might want to try.

A collection of assorted skunks.

Painting More Animals on Rocks

How to Paint a
Beaver

Perhaps you'll be eager as a beaver to try your hand at these winsome, industrious critters. Begin by looking for oval rocks. The ideal rock is shaped like a giant jelly bean with one flat side serving as the base. As with all the animals in this book, beavers can be done in a vast range of sizes. You may even come across a rock that lends itself to a sitting up pose. The rock I selected is a standard shape, similar to the semicircle skunk rock, but not so narrow since beavers are more roly-poly. As always, make sure your rock is scrubbed clean before going on.

A few assorted beaver rocks. Their shared characteristics are the blunt shapes and chubby contours.

Here's the fourth rock from the above group: an ordinary oval shape that will do nicely.

Here are three of those rocks with sketched-on features. Do you see the difference between the crouched animals and the one sitting up in the middle?

1 Base Coat

Cover the entire rock except for the very bottom with a base coat of dark brown. Use a premixed shade, or make your own by starting with a good-sized puddle of Burnt Sienna and adding enough black to create a rich, chocolate syrup color. A large brush will allow you to apply a solid coat quickly.

2 Layout

When the base coat has thoroughly dried, use a piece of chalk or a white-lead pencil to sketch in your beaver's features.

Select the smoothest, most uniform end of your rock for the head. Start by making a circle there, taking up as much as one-third of the rock. Ideally, this circle should leave just enough room below the chin for the front paws.

Next, sketch an oval nose in the center of the head. The beaver's small eyes should be spaced far apart (at least four eye-widths), and set approximately halfway between the nose and the top of the face circle. Small, rounded ears line up with the eye circles, creating a diagonal line from nose to ear. Below the nose, draw a short, straight line, then curve muzzle lines off on either side. Sketch in two oversized front teeth that slightly overlap a short, semi-circle chin to finish sketching in the face.

Tuck two simple paw shapes with long fingers under the chin. To complete the rest of the layout, draw a circular haunch that takes up slightly more than the rear third of the rock on either side. Keep these haunch circles about the same height as the ears. Place long, flipper-like feet below the front edge of the haunch. The recommended length of the feet depends on the shape of your rock, but allow the toes to taper off before reaching the front paws. Check to make sure that your beaver's facial features are symmetrical and uniform and that the eyes are level. Once you're satisfied, you're ready to begin painting.

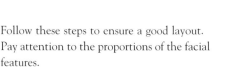

Follow these steps to ensure a good layout. Pay attention to the proportions of the facial features.

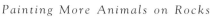

Painting More Animals on Rocks

Cover the rock with a base coat of dark brown paint, then sketch the layout in with white chalk.

These sketches show several possible poses—standing, head up and head down.

3 Contours

A beaver's coloring is a subtle blend of browns. Begin by selecting a medium-sized brush with short, stiff bristles. Use it to scrub Burnt Sienna highlights along your contour lines. Start around the face, drawing each short stroke outward to create a fringe circling the head, skipping past the ears.

Next, use more Burnt Sienna to highlight the curves of the haunches. Keep your strokes angled down and back in the same streamlined manner that a beaver's fur grows. Indicate the upper portion of the front leg between the face and haunch. Finally, working from the top, highlight two crescent-shaped shoulder areas.

Now switch to a smaller, round brush and black paint. Fill in the centers of the ears first, then the eye circles. Finally, darken in two nostril holes about the same diameter as the eyes. Still using black, paint the rear feet on both sides.

4 Fur

Because beaver fur is not very showy, the textured look you create with your details is especially important. Use a liner brush and Yellow Ochre to modify all previously highlighted areas. Start with a fringe of fur strokes bordering the head circle. Vary the length and spacing and even the color of these strokes by interspersing touches of Yellow Ochre lightened a shade with white or darkened with Burnt Sienna. Scatter a semicircle of strokes beneath each eye as well. Move on to the haunch circles, and make the same kinds of lines, always angling your strokes to follow the natural growth pattern of the fur. Fur lines should be denser along the top and sparser along the bottom of the haunch circle. Loosen up and allow your strokes to have a random look.

These guidelines ensure that your brushstrokes follow the natural direction in which a beaver's coat grows.

Burnt Sienna brushstrokes applied with a large, stiff brush create contrast and highlight contours. Fill in the centers of the ears, the eye circles, the nostrils and the flipper-like rear feet with black. Heighten the contrast by blending Yellow Ochre fur lines over the previous layer of Burnt Sienna.

Defining the muzzle areas with lighter paint to make them stand out is vital on an animal that is basically monochromatic.

Painting More Animals on Rocks

After the haunch, highlight the shoulders and indicate the line of the beaver's front legs. Add detail to the back of the rock, too, so that there are no large, unbroken patches of plain brown.

Next, extend some short, eyelash-like lines up from the top curve of the eyes. Scatter fur lines over the forehead as well, and into the cheek areas below the eyes.

Lighten your Yellow Ochre with white and use this color to define the muzzle areas, fanning out several overlapping sets of short lines to create half circles extending from either side of the nose. Continue to darken and lighten your strokes with varying combinations of white, Yellow Ochre and Burnt Sienna as you layer on more fur lines, building up successive rows of fur.

While you have a lighter combination of Yellow Ochre and white on your brush, outline the ear and eye circles to bring them into focus. Go over the top double curve of the nose to help it stand out. At the same time, fill in the squared front teeth shapes. A series of short, dense lines will also help define the chin below the teeth. Avoid painting over the dark outlines between the features.

To add yet another dimension to the beaver's fur, switch now to straight Burnt Sienna and scatter reddish brown highlights in among the other shades.

Add layer upon layer of paint to build up fur lines in varying shades all over the face.

Use a pale off-white to bring out the shape of the ears, define the eyes and add emphasis to the nose and muzzle area. Paint in the square teeth and indicate the curve of the chin behind the teeth with this color.

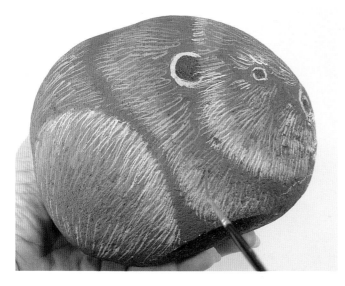

Scatter Burnt Sienna fur lines among the lighter fur lines, but concentrate most of them in the less detailed, darker areas.

5 Finishing Touches

Now you're ready to add the final small touches that will complete this piece. To finish the rear feet, mix white and black to get a small amount of gray paint. Leaving dark outlines in place, use gray to indicate three long, tapering toes. For the stubbier front paws, use a combination of Yellow Ochre and Burnt Sienna to indicate fingers, again leaving darker paint in place between each finger for definition. While you're working near the face, look to see if you need to refine any of the facial features by darkening the outlines around them. When every area of your beaver looks finished, add tiny dots of white paint to the eyes for a lifelike sparkle. Allow the paint to dry.

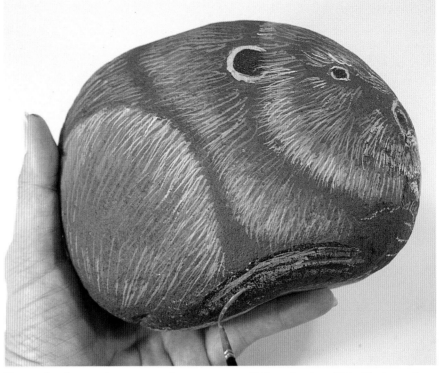

Use streaks of gray paint to create the appearance of light reflecting off the black rear feet.

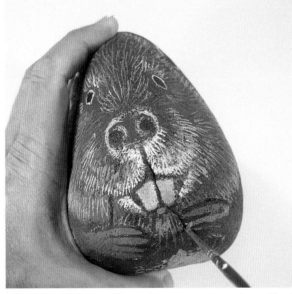

Mix Yellow Ochre and Burnt Sienna to paint in the stubby fingers of the front paws so that they stand out against their darker background.

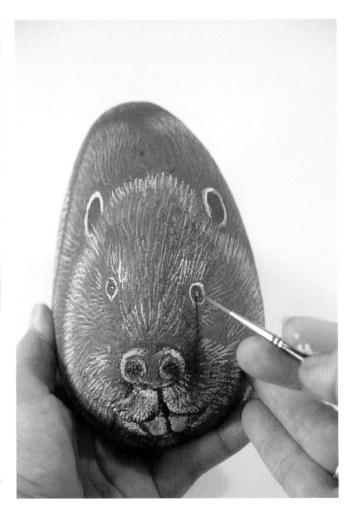

Touch up outlines to make sure all your beaver's features are clearly defined. As always, a small dot of white in each eye seems to bring your rock creation to life.

Painting More Animals on Rocks

6 Creating a Tail

None of the beaver's features is quite as distinctive as the large, flat tail. A scrap of leather makes a perfect tail. Generally, the tail should be no bigger than the diameter of the rock's base. Baby beavers have even smaller tails in proportion to body size. Remember to extend the front flap of the tail at least 3″ to 4″ (7.6cm to 10.2cm) so you can attach that part to the underside of the rock.

After you cut the tail shape out, paint it a dark brown that is almost black. When it's dry, attach it with wood filler or a household glue. When you spray the rock with polyurethane, make sure to coat the surface of the tail as well.

If you don't have access to scrap leather, try using denim or some other heavy fabric. Sew two oval layers together, remembering to add a tab that's 2″ to 3″ (5.1cm to 7.6cm) long to one end so you can attach it. Turn the stitching inside out and paint the tail a dark black-brown. Allow it to dry before attaching it to the bottom rear portion of your rock. You can also use a single layer of heavy fabric; just be sure to finish off the cut edge with dark fabric paint to prevent the material from fraying or unraveling.

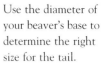

Use the diameter of your beaver's base to determine the right size for the tail.

Cut out the tail, leaving an extra flap where you'll glue it to the bottom of the beaver. If it's a light color, or if you're using fabric, paint the tail with dark paint before you attach it.

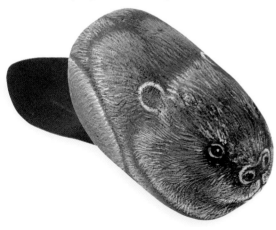

A finished beaver, ready to chew down a tree.

Here's a whole colony of assorted beavers.

Painting More Animals on Rocks

How to Paint a
Squirrel

If you've ever been entertained by the antics of these cheeky little acrobats, I hope you'll agree that squirrels are as much fun to paint as they are to watch. When selecting squirrel rocks, keep in mind that full, fluffy tails are their hallmark. To be suitable, a rock must have enough height to allow such a tail to curve and bend over the animal's back. The nearly square rock I picked for this project offers plenty of room for the tail, and it's wide enough without being as rotund as a beaver.

Any of these rocks will work; note the nicely rounded tops.

What You'll Need

- acrylic paints in black, white, Burnt Sienna, Yellow Ochre (Antique Gold or Harvest Gold can be substituted anywhere Yellow Ochre is used) and red
- chalk or a white-lead pencil
- assorted brushes

I liked the almost square shape of this rock because it provided ample tail room.

1 Base Coat

Once you've chosen your rock, make sure the surface is scrubbed clean. Begin this project by painting the entire surface of the rock black. A large brush will make for quick coverage.

2 Layout

When the paint is dry, use chalk or a white-lead pencil to sketch in the details. As with the skunk, situate the head so that the squirrel seems to be looking back over its body. On occasion it's possible to come across rock shapes that allow head placement at one end, but rocks for the pose I demonstrate are much more common. Keep the placement of the head fairly low to insure plenty of room for the tail.

A squirrel's head is basically a tilting egg shape, with the smaller, lower end as the muzzle. Try to keep the size of the head in proportion to the size of the rock; make the head too large and your squirrel will look like a cartoon animal. A head that's too small is less distracting than one that's too big. Generally, the head should take up about 25 percent of the side surface of the rock.

Divide the head oval in half lengthwise (following the degree of tilt you gave it) and set one pointy ear at the top, so the inside edge of the ear lines up with the dividing line. Center a large round eye at the midpoint of that line and sketch in a **Y**-shaped nose at the bottom of the oval. Next, sketch in a slightly larger oval haunch set lengthwise across from the head.

Curve the tail up, beginning along the back edge of the haunch and angling it forward over the body in a gentle arc, stopping just above the head. Double the tail back upon itself and taper your line inward to form a folded-over tip. Turn the rock around and copy the curved lines on the other side to complete a fat, flowing tail.

Start by applying a solid black base coat.

These illustrations show various rock shapes and possible layout options.

Painting More Animals on Rocks

Finish your layout by tucking rear feet at the bottom edge of the rock where the haunch curves in. Make the rear feet narrow and elongated, with simple toes curving down. The front feet extend forward below the head, with shorter, more rounded paws and the suggestion of bending elbows. Don't forget to sketch the rear view of these features on the back side as well.

Look your layout over to make sure the proportions seem balanced before going on. Remember that you can brush or wash away any marks that don't look right and simply try again.

Your layout may differ depending on the rock you chose, but note how the head, haunch, tail and feet compare proportionally to one another.

3 Fur

A medium-sized round bristled brush is a good choice for scrubbing in the white patches that set off the curves of the haunches all the way down to and including the rear feet. Then fill in the chest area below the head and between the front paws. If the bristles of your round brush are stiff enough for the strokes to suggest individual fur clumps, use it to outline the tail, too. If not, switch to a liner brush to create the desired fuzzy look with a series of short strokes.

Check the fur directional chart to help determine how your strokes should slant for a natural look. Define the edges of the ears and the curve of the head with short, spiky fur lines.

Now you're ready to cover the entire squirrel with more of these short, splinter-like fur marks that will give the animal its realistic texture. Begin along the top edge of the haunch and layer in successive rows of tiny white strokes, varying both the length and spacing

Crisp white patches of fur on the edges of the haunch and on the chest are an important element in your squirrel's design.

and allowing some strokes to angle or cross others. When you have filled in the haunch areas on both sides, move to the head. Since the fur grows from the tip of the nose upward, you may want to hold the rock upside down to

facilitate your strokes. Pay close attention to the way fur looks around the muzzle and below the eye.

After the head and haunch are filled in, move to the side area between them and again follow the fur directional guide in detailing this space. Leave a narrow border of black in place to outline the head, haunch and tail and make them stand out. When the front side is complete, move to the area behind the head and work your way around the curve of the rock to the other side. Since the head doesn't show on this side, the fur lines should continue along the back as well as angling downward to form the upper portion of the other front leg. Outline the back rear foot with spiky little strokes too.

Use this guide to determine the direction the fur grows on various parts of a squirrel.

Painting More Animals on Rocks

Delicate fur lines will give your squirrel realistic texture. Keep them short and fairly dense. When adding fur, always leave dark borders around your main features to make them stand out. Continue fur lines above the head and around to the back side of the rock.

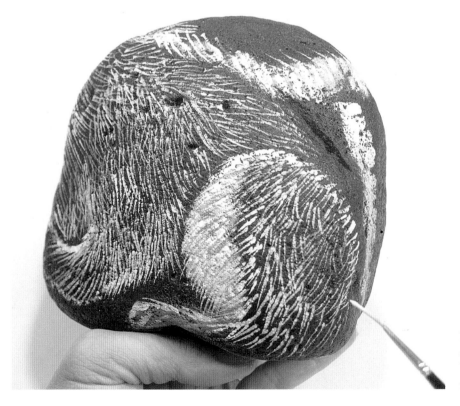

Pay special attention to the subtle change of direction which some fur follows along the back. Some fur angles downward to fill in the front leg.

This three-step illustration should help you
master the facial fur detailing.

Painting More Animals on Rocks

4 Details

Switch to a larger round or square brush and mix equal parts of Yellow Ochre and Burnt Sienna. Add enough water to this mixture to create a translucent wash that will tint your white strokes without altering the darker tones. You may want to try a test area to check the effect. If your tint is too strong, it will dull down the black undercoat. If so, use a paper towel to blot it away and try again with a looser mixture. The idea behind tinting the fur is to add visual interest, so use it sparingly here and there. Leave some fur lines white, particularly those along the outside edges of the head and haunch. Remember to tint the back side fur as well.

Now return to your liner brush and add enough white paint to your golden brown tint mixture to get a pale gold color. If the pigment is too watery, you may need to add more Yellow Ochre. Use this soft gold to add details to the fluffy tail. Start at the bottom back edge of the rock and angle your strokes upward and outward along the base of the tail, leaving a dark "part" down the center. Move to the folded-over tail tip, working upward from the tapering end. Allow your strokes to grow longer and more flowing as they extend along either side of the tail's top.

Tinting portions of the squirrel's fur is an easy way to add natural looking shading, but don't go overboard with it. Leave areas of white, particularly around the edges.

Use pale gold to create the look of fluffy tail fur. See how I left a dark part in the center?

Switch to straight Burnt Sienna and scatter some reddish fur lines in among the golden ones, occasionally overlapping into the fringe of white tail fur. Also use this color to fill in the small **U**-shaped nose.

For the ears, use a small, rounded brush and mix up a medium shade of gray, adding a touch of red paint to create a dusky pink color. Dab it into the ears carefully, leaving just a suggestion of darker paint in place between it and the white ear outlines.

Change to your liner brush and black paint to fill in the eye circle next.

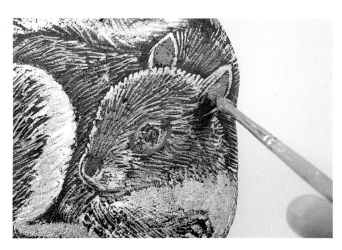

Use an understated shade of pink to fill in the ears. Leave a bit of dark border between the pink centers and the white outline.

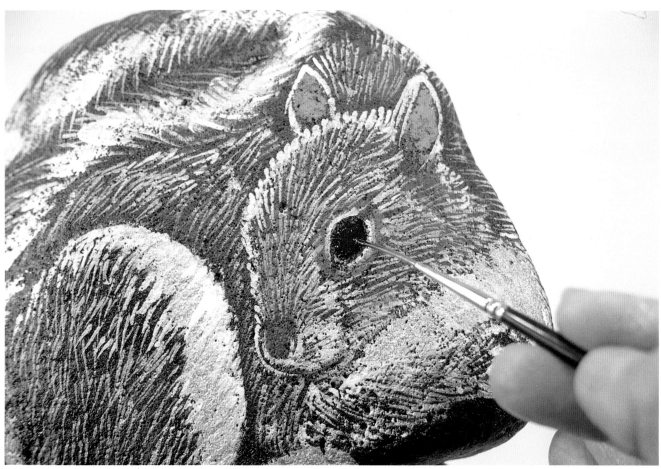

Contrasting strokes of Burnt Sienna help define the tail and add a reddish hue.

Fill the eye in with solid black paint.

Painting More Animals on Rocks

5 Finishing Touches

While you have black on your brush, this is a good time to target areas of your squirrel that may need more emphasis or definition. Look for places where fur strokes may have obscured the underlying features. On my piece the front leg and paw were too indistinct. I remedied this by adding new dark lines of fur to the top of the leg, making it stand out from the white chest area. Other places that seemed to need more detail included the curve of the haunch and the tail. When in doubt, it rarely hurts to add a few dark accents to clean up white fur lines that look too thick or to add emphasis.

Note how a few dark strokes sharply redefine the front leg.

Scatter additional dark fur strokes where needed to create even more realistic detail. Pay attention to the inside edges of white bordering the tail.

Complete the eye by adding a touch of Burnt Sienna to the black on your brush and using this deep shade to make a half circle around the side and bottom of the eye. Leaving the center black creates the look of an iris.

Returning to black, add just enough water to insure that the paint flows easily without becoming transparent. Carefully stroke in five or six slightly arching whiskers, beginning inside the muzzle area and flowing gracefully outward. Add a tiny dot or two of white to make the eye sparkle. As always, a coat of polyurethane will seal the surface and bring out the rich colors.

A scant semicircle of dark brown adds realistic depth to the eye.

Narrow black whiskers frame the squirrel's face. Don't they look like they're just about to twitch?

A double dot of white adds a mischievous glint to this squirrel's eye.

Check your creation from every angle to make sure you've got enough detail and definition. Does he look lonely? Maybe you need to paint a friend for him.

Painting More Animals on Rocks

More Ideas . . .

One variation you might want to try
is a mama squirrel with a youngster.

Some other design variations.

A mama squirrel posed with her baby makes
an appealing subject.

Painting More Animals on Rocks

How to Paint a
Calf

One of the joys of country living is the sight of brand new calves curled up in lush spring grass. But you don't have to have a rural address to own an adorable little calf. I've chosen to paint a baby Holstein because they are the most common and collectible breed of cow, but you can adapt the instructions to other kinds if you prefer.

When searching for suitable rocks for this project, look for plump oval shapes. You might even come across one with a slightly angular end which could be adapted as a bent back leg. Avoid flat rocks, since calves are rather lumpy looking creatures. Wash your rock and let it dry.

Any of these rocks would be a good choice. The tan spot on the right rear rock is where I filled a small hole with wood filler.

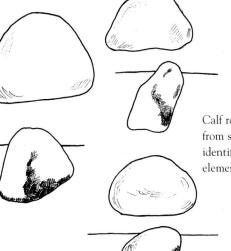

Calf rock shapes from several angles identify the elements to look for.

Here are the same rocks after I sketched on possible layouts, demonstrating the variety of looks you can achieve.

I liked this rock for its height and smooth surface. The rock you choose could be smaller—or much larger—but this is a good size for a first try.

1 Layout

Before you begin, try to envision a calf's broad features on your particular rock. To be in proper proportion, the head should take up no more than 30 to 40 percent of the top and front surfaces.

A primary consideration when sketching your initial layout is that you allow enough room for the ears. It's okay if the outside ear curves slightly around the corner of the stone, but too much of a curve will make it seem to vanish, leaving your animal looking lopsided. Since the ears lie in an almost straight line with the top of the calf's head, start by sketching the outside ear as an elongated oval with a slightly pointed tip. Join that ear to a larger oval, perhaps twice as wide across as the ear is long. This will be the forehead.

Create a matching ear opposite the first. At this point check to see that your head is set to one side, not directly in the center of the rock. If it is in the middle, erase your sketch marks and move it over, making the head smaller if needed.

Once the top of the head looks right, place your pencil or marker just inside the lower curve of the forehead oval and draw a tapering line from either side. These lines should be no longer than the forehead oval is high. To form the muzzle, sketch a much smaller oval at the end of the tapering face lines, letting the sides of the muzzle bulge out slightly beyond the straight face lines.

Set eye circles along the lower outside curves of the forehead oval. Large, widely spaced eyes are characteristic of calves—make sure that there is at least a three-eye-width distance between the inside corners of the two eyes.

The nose is essentially a triangle shape that takes up a substantial portion of the muzzle oval. The two upper angles are pointed, while the bottom

Basic geometric shapes make layout easy. Paying careful attention to the proportions will keep the features in balance.

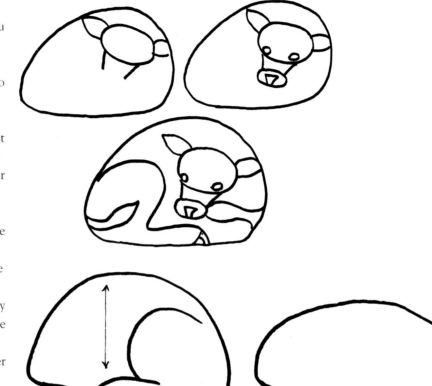

Depending on the shape of your rock, you may not need to sketch features on the back side.

By tilting the head slightly, I provided a bit more room for the outside ear. Use a pencil first, then go back over your lines with marker when you're ready.

Painting More Animals on Rocks

one is wider and squared off.

After the facial features are in place, the rest of the layout is easy. Create a rounded haunch shape opposite the head, and sketch in a bent back leg with a split hoof along the bottom of the rock as shown.

Depending on how much space there is, sketch a folded front leg under the chin, with a rounded end to suggest a knee. Tuck a second folded front leg on the other side. Run a curving line from under the head down to just above the front leg, representing the calf's neck. Then form a narrow tail shape that curves around from the end of the rock and ends with a small tassel.

Depending on your rock's shape, you may or may not want to define any features on the rear side of the rock. If you do, all you need to indicate is the curving oval of the other haunch.

Outline the shape of the white blaze, beginning with the muzzle and going up the center of the face before broadening out on the forehead.

2 Base Coat

Once you are satisfied with your layout, begin painting. Start with plain white paint and a medium-sized square or round brush. Fill in the haunch first and then the rest of the body, leaving your guidelines uncovered. Don't panic if you accidentally paint over any part of these lines—they are only there to help you remember your layout, so just resketch them when the paint dries. Since much of the face will be black, paint only the muzzle and face blaze. Also paint the back side of your rock and around the sides down to the bottom edge.

In order to create dimension, mix a medium-to-dark shade of gray paint and use it to shade around the outside edges of the head and the outside curves of the haunches. Go around the

When blocking in the white areas of your calf, try not to paint over your guidelines. Paint the body, tail and blaze, leaving the rest of the head unpainted.

Gray shadows around the head will make it stand out. Note how my strokes radiate out and away from the head as I go around it. Use gray to go over the rest of your guidelines, too.

How to Paint a Calf   69

legs and tail with gray outlines, too, and use gray to make the neckline stand out.

Switch to black paint and begin by painting irregular splotches on the haunch, leg, back and other side of the rock. These markings can be just like mine, or you can create your own unique combination. Use the black to accentuate the curve of the haunch and

the lines of the tail. Blending black above the crook of the rear leg will add to the impression of depth and dimension.

Outline around the ears and nose, then paint the remaining portions of the head, leaving the eye circles, centers of the ears and nose unpainted.

Mix a small amount of white paint with a little red to get a medium shade

of pink. Add a touch of black to soften it to a subdued, dusky pink, and use this color to fill in the nose area. Use the same pink to fill in the insides of the ears and the split hoof showing in front.

Use Burnt Sienna darkened with a touch of black to paint the eyes. Now there should be no unpainted areas left on your calf.

Your black markings will look more natural if you vary the sizes and keep the edges irregular. Next, fill in the head shape and outline the ears. Darken the shadows right above the bent rear leg to increase the illusion of contour.

Red, white and a touch of black produce a dusky pink that's just right for the nose, the insides of the ears and the hoof.

Mix Burnt Sienna with a tiny amount of black and use this deep brown color to fill in the circles of the eyes.

Painting More Animals on Rocks

To ensure that your details look realistic and natural, use this directional guide whenever you add fur lines.

3 Fur

Switch to a liner brush and black paint. Extend a row of longer fur lines down from the upper edges of each ear. Create shorter, fringe-like fur lines along the bottom ear edges. Give the curve of the haunch a defining set of short, prickly lines, then begin adding little fur lines to the splotches. The fur directional chart will help you decide how the detailing fur lines should be placed. Other areas that need added details include the end of the tail, the tops of the legs, around the outsides of the ears and around the head. Use tiny black lines to soften the blaze and the curve of the muzzle. Don't neglect the spots on the back side of your rock.

Finally, place black iris ovals in the centers of each eye.

Begin your black fur details on the insides of the ears. Tiny black lines give texture to the curve of the haunch. Extend these prickly looking lines all the way down along the rear leg, then add them to the top of the front legs.

4 Gray Highlights

Using the same liner brush, mix up a medium shade of gray paint and use it to soften the black portions of your calf. On the markings, add clusters of highlighting lines, paying particular attention to the areas bordering the curve of the haunch. Make sure these highlighting lines follow the same general direction used for the black fur lines. On the calf's back, concentrate the most dense rows of highlighting along the edges of the spots that face toward the head, then scatter more random lines around the centers and other edges.

Use these gray details to better define the shaded area between the head and haunch, again using the directional chart to angle your strokes the way fur would naturally grow.

Gray fur lines are an especially important element in detailing the face and ears. On the ears, place them between the dark fur fringes painted earlier. For the face, use a narrow gray line to highlight the bottom curve of the eye, then stroke in dense sets of lines to help suggest realistic curves and contours. Leave dark borders around any such lines for contrast and definition. The deeper gray shading behind the calf's head also needs to be softened and redefined by these lighter gray lines, as does the area below the head and along the neckline.

Turn your rock around and add touches of gray fur to the spots on the back side, concentrating them along the top edges of the spots and scattering them elsewhere.

This close-up look at the face shows how highlighting lines work together to give the head the realistic look of planes and angles.

These gray highlights should be densest around the edges of the haunches and more scattered and random elsewhere. Use dense lines to define and detail the shaded area between the head and haunch. Change the angle and density of your strokes as you work around the head. A narrow underlining of gray below the curve of each eye will make them stand out.

Painting More Animals on Rocks

Add narrow gray lines around the borders of your shaded areas to lend visual interest. This includes the narrow strip of shading directly above the head.

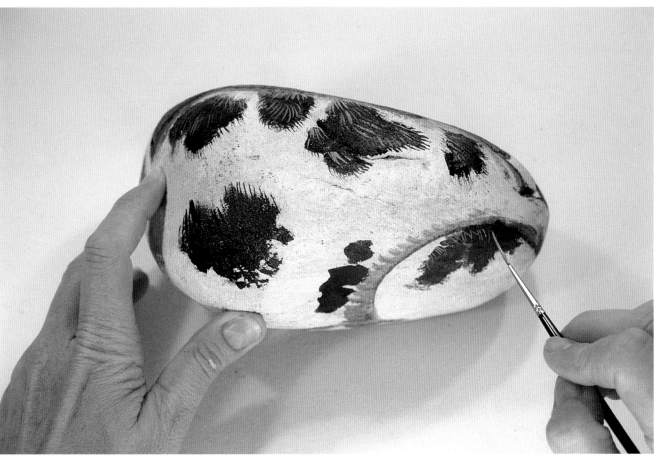

It's easy to neglect the back side, but a few gray highlights are all that are needed.

5 Finishing Touches

There are many small but important details that will give your calf the polished look of a finished piece. Start by mixing a brushful of Burnt Sienna with a bit of black paint to darken it to a deep brown shade. Use this color to outline the shape of the nose, then add a few lines in the center between the nostrils. While you have Burnt Sienna on your palette, add a ring of it to the outside edge of the eye for more warmth and depth. Rinse out your brush and mix up very small amounts of several shades of gray. Use these to detail the muzzle area as shown.

Outlining and shading the nose with dark brown gives it more definition.

A simple ring of Burnt Sienna inside the bottom half of the eyes warms them up.

Painting More Animals on Rocks

Switch to white paint to add the curved sliver of a lower lip below the muzzle area. While you have white on your brush, place the bright gleams in the calf's eyes, horizontally centering them in the top half of the black irises.

Add a cluster or two of white fur to the neckline, white highlights to detail the top of the tail tip and some white lines sprouting down from the upper edges of the ears.

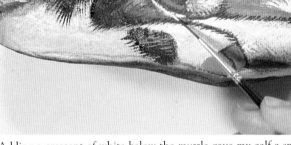

Small details in shades of gray liven up the muzzle area.

Adding a crescent of white below the muzzle gave my calf a small, contented smile.

Bright white double gleams in the eyes seem to bring them to life. Additional touches of white add interest to the neck, highlight the tail fur and fill the ears.

Use soft gray paint to create the look of a whorl in the center of the calf's white face blaze, then sprinkle a few straight gray lines just above the nose. Use this gray and your liner brush to add details to the white areas on your calf's haunch as well as along the curve of the back—and anywhere else that looks unfinished and needs a bit of touching up. You can add as much or as little detail as you want to the white areas, but I recommend leaving some areas mostly white, particularly the top of the haunch, the center of the back and the shoulders above the head.

This whorl on the calf's forehead is like a star with curving points. Note how a few straight lines just above the nose add more interesting detail.

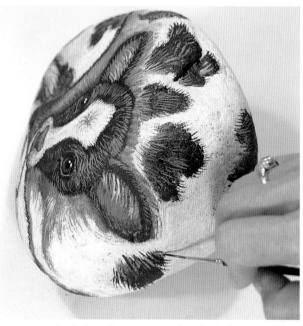

It's easy to overlook the side areas since they don't show from the front. A few gray fur lines create the desired effect.

Pale gray fur lines scattered between the calf's markings on the lower haunch and back lend yet another layer of texture and detail.

Painting More Animals on Rocks

More Ideas . . .

I used photographs from farm magazines to paint other breeds of calves, including a white-faced Hereford and a doe-eyed Brown Swiss. As my herd grew I began to feel almost like a cattle rancher! Rock calves make great gift ideas for dairy farmers, cattle ranchers and anyone else who appreciates these country critters.

Watchful and alert, this calf seems to have a life of its own!

Here are the same calves shown as plain rocks at the beginning of this demo. They look even more at home on a bed of freshly cut grass.

Painting More Animals on Rocks

How to Paint a
Foal

A newborn foal makes a wonderful addition to any menagerie of rock animals. It's a great gift for horse lovers, too. Best of all, foals are surprisingly simple to paint. Good foal rocks come in a variety of easy-to-find shapes. They can be painted on plain, plump oval rocks or on ones whose tapering ends suggest the sharp crook of a folded rear leg. Foal rocks can also be semicircular and sit up on their flat end like the rock I've picked to demonstrate this project. Remember to scrub the rock before going on.

What You'll Need

- acrylic paints in black, white, Burnt Sienna and Yellow Ochre (Antique Gold or Harvest Gold may be substituted anywhere Yellow Ochre is used)
- pencil or marker
- assorted brushes

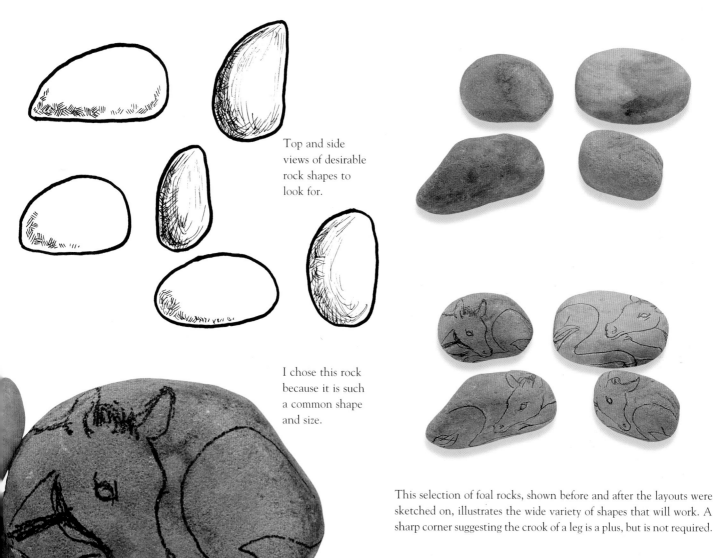

Top and side views of desirable rock shapes to look for.

I chose this rock because it is such a common shape and size.

This selection of foal rocks, shown before and after the layouts were sketched on, illustrates the wide variety of shapes that will work. A sharp corner suggesting the crook of a leg is a plus, but is not required.

Sketching in your foal's features step by step.

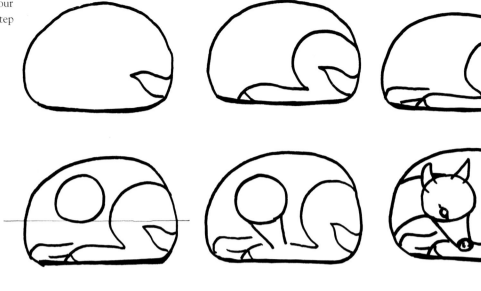

1 Layout

To determine the best layout for your particular rock, decide where the rear leg would look best. On my rock, one side was quite rounded. The other side looked irregular, but there was no definite crook. Sweeping the tail in just above a tightly-folded rear leg helps disguise the lack of a distinctive angle. Next, curve a rounded haunch into place above it, taking up a little less than half the front surface of the rock. Extend the lower part of the leg along the bottom of the rock, ending it with a curving hoof. The suggestion of a folded front leg is achieved by sketching in a rounded knee at the base of the head end, then running the leg line back toward the middle.

A horse's head can be broken down into three basic shapes. First, make a circle that is slightly smaller in diameter than the top curve of the haunch. Position this circle so that its bottom edge is halfway above the base of the rock. Taper two straight lines off the head circle, with the outside line even with the curve of the head circle, while the inside line is slightly indented. These two lines should measure no more than the diameter of the head circle, and ease toward each other until

they are half as far apart as when they began. Join them with a semicircular muzzle. It may take you more than one try to get the proportions just right, so be patient.

Next, sketch two pointed ears, one on either side atop the head circle and with about an ear width between their bases. Add two nostrils to the muzzle and place the eye at the bottom edge of the head circle as shown.

Another important feature is the broad, arching neck. Curve a line back from the top center point of the head to the edge of the rock, then swing it back in a **C**-shape following the imagined spine of your foal. The lower neck line should curve around the end of the rock and stop just past where you placed the front knee. Sketch a second knee and leg that comes around from the other side. If it's an upright rock, indicate a second haunch on the back side with a tucked-in rear leg and hoof. Finally, add a few spiky lines between the ears and along the neck to indicate a short mane.

Compare your layout to mine and make any adjustments needed. Now you're ready to begin painting.

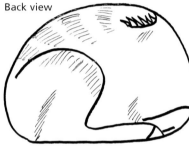

Back view

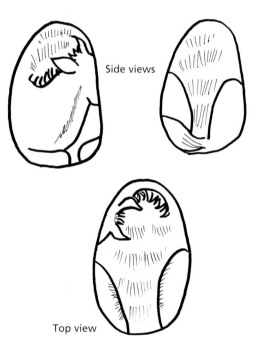

Side views

Top view

Painting More Animals on Rocks

2 Base Coat

Use a medium-sized brush and black paint to outline all the features you just sketched, then darken the area between the head and haunch, and shade the area directly below the head and along the bottom edge of the neck. Turn the rock around and outline the back features, too. Don't forget to outline the bottom edges of the legs to help define them.

Next, mix Burnt Sienna and black paint together to get a deep brown. You can use the same brush you used for the outlines, or switch to a bigger one. Blend this deep brown into the edges of your black shadows, then use it to completely cover the top of the foal and around the back side, leaving the head, neck, haunches and legs unpainted.

Rinse your brush or switch to a slightly smaller one and use straight Burnt Sienna to paint the head, neck, haunches and legs. Leave a blaze-shaped area on the face unpainted.

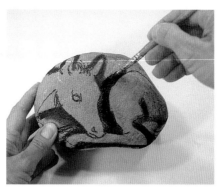

Bold black outlines suggest the illusion of contours.

This deep brown background will help the head and haunches stand out.

See how this warm reddish-brown color seems to pull the head and haunch forward?

How to Paint a Foal

81

A white face blaze and one white sock are welcome additions to the overall design.

Use black to emphasize the eyes, nostrils, mouth and mane.

With a smaller brush, add a crisp white blaze and one white sock. Switch to black paint to outline the shape of the eye, fill in the nostrils and indicate the mouth with a simple straight line. Color in the tail and create a tuft of mane between the ears.

Mix a bit more deep brown paint to fill in the eye circle and darken the insides of the ears.

Fill in both the eye and the centers of the ears with dark brown.

Painting More Animals on Rocks

3 Contours

To add to the illusion of contour and to give the foal's coat a sheen, use a stubby round brush (one of those worn out brushes you were about to throw away is perfect). Mix Yellow Ochre with just a touch of white and use this to highlight the sides of your foal's face, the entire top and inside edge of the haunch all the way down to the rear leg and along the top of the leg. On the underside of the head use small, more distinct strokes to add emphasis continuing past the line of the neck to highlight the semicircular curve of the jaw line. Then add a simple line from the top of that curve down toward where the neck joins the chest, indicating a prominent muscle there. Highlight the top of the front leg as well. Turn the stone around and add the same highlighting touches to the back side.

With a smaller brush and a slightly paler shade of gold, outline the pointed ears. Highlight the bump indicating the unseen eye, then encircle the outside eye with light gold. Note that the bottom of this eye highlighting is a simple half circle, while the upper half sweeps up in the direction of the ear.

Scrubbing in touches of gold adds a lifelike sheen to your foal's coat. Make them denser along the haunch and leg, more subtle on the head and neck.

A smaller brush and lighter gold frames the eye nicely. Use it on the bump above the unseen eye as well, and to outline around the ears.

4 Finishing Touches

With your liner brush mix a small amount of deep gray paint and use it to highlight the tuft of mane between the ears and to add a few sweeping lines to the tail. Carefully fill in the muzzle around the nostrils and the mouth.

Turn the rock around and add a row of short, spiky lines to the mane along the arch of the neck. Finally, add an outline of gray to the shape of the hoof to define it.

Gray paint covers the end of the muzzle and creates contrast when stroked on as a highlight along the mane and tail. Turn your rock if necessary to highlight the mane along the arch of the neck. Use gray to define the shape of the hoof.

Rinse out your liner brush and squeeze out one drop each of white, Yellow Ochre and Burnt Sienna on your palette. Pick up a touch of white on your brush tip, then a touch of Yellow Ochre. Mix them and check the texture with a test stroke to see if you'll need to add water so your strokes will go on cleanly. Use the fur directional guide to add numerous small, splintery fur lines to the face, neck, haunch and legs. Add a few lines to the insides of the ears, too. As you paint these fur lines, vary the combination of colors to achieve a subtle, random look as you scatter them around.

When you detail the upper portion of the neck and the darker areas like the back and sides, use a darker blend of Burnt Sienna with occasional golden touches here and there. Fur lines can be less dense in these darker areas. Along the back and in the shaded side areas, use a dry brush and straight Burnt Sienna to indicate less distinct sets of lines.

After you have added the texture of fur to all the areas mentioned, clean your brush and switch to black paint to add an iris to the eye. Look for other areas that may need clearer definition as well. On my piece I felt the muzzle area could use a bit more work. I darkened the center between the nostrils, then surrounded them with lighter outlines for accent.

Use this fur directional guide to help determine how your detailing strokes should look.

Golden fur lines should be densest near the edges of the haunch. Use sparser streaks around the face and along the tops of the legs. Sprinkle a few in the ears, as well.

Switch to Burnt Sienna to add a set of dry brushed lines to the chest area below the neck. Move on to dry brush more of these diffused lines along the top, back and sides. Small black details such as the iris, more clearly defined nostril shapes and a sharp mouth line are also important additions.

How to Paint a Foal

To give the eye more depth, I encircled the outermost edge with a narrow line of lighter brown.

In looking my foal over, I concluded that more fur lines, this time in a dark brown, would be useful. The areas I targeted for this treatment included the neck just above the muscle line I'd highlighted earlier, the area around the base of the outside ear, the eye area below the gold highlighting and the areas along both sides of the blaze. I also added darker fur lines to the haunch, slightly in from the outside edge and curving to suggest the substantial nature of that muscled area. Then I added a row of dark detailing lines to the lower side of the legs to emphasize the look of shading along them.

Finally, place one or two tiny dots of white in the upper portion of the eye.

Look your piece over from every angle to be sure you've added enough detail. Pay special attention to the base of the neck and to the tail's base, both of which are easily overlooked.

An outside rim of lighter brown gives the eye a warm glow.

Blending dark fur lines among the lighter ones will give your foal even more texture and contour. Concentrate on the entire lower edge of the rear leg, the lower portion of the folded front leg, the areas under the eye and above the highlighted muscle along the neck. Add some dark lines right behind the ear, too, then move to the haunch to detail the area just above the tail. Scatter a few more dark lines just inside the curve of the haunch to give it bulk. A star-shaped cluster of lines in the center of the face blaze gives the look of a whorl.

Painting More Animals on Rocks

Add a couple of bright gleams in the eye and your foal is complete.

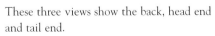

These three views show the back, head end and tail end.

How to Paint a Foal

More Ideas . . .

Foals are particularly appealing posed on a bit of hay or dried grass. I even painted a standing mama horse to nuzzle my foal, shown on page 78, blacking out the rock to suggest spaces between her legs.

The finished foal.

Painting More Animals on Rocks

These variations of the foal we just painted
look right at home nestled in a bed of straw.

Painting More Animals on Rocks

How to Paint a
Bear

E ver since the original teddy bear cinched their popularity, bears have been favored by collectors, and treasured by generations of youngsters. Here is yet another way to capture their singular charm.

A sitting-up pose is the most logical way to interpret the roly-poly physique, the broad head and, of course, those bear feet. Look for rocks that are shaped something like a rounded headstone: upright on flat bottoms and taller than they are wide. The top can be quite blunt or taper somewhat, but rocks that are too pointed won't have enough room for widely spaced ears.

The rock I'm using for this demonstration is an almost perfect "headstone," flat bottomed and gently curved on top. The sample layouts for a variety of rocks illustrate the fact that many different sizes and shapes of rocks will work.

What You'll Need

- acrylic paints in black, Nutmeg Brown, Burnt Sienna, Yellow Ochre (Antique Gold or Harvest Gold can be substituted anywhere Yellow Ochre is used) and white
- pencil or marker
- assorted brushes

See how the same basic layout adapts to many different shapes and sizes of rocks?

Look for rocks like these. Note the bluntness of the tops and the way all these rocks sit sturdily on flat bottoms.

Here's my choice for a great bear.

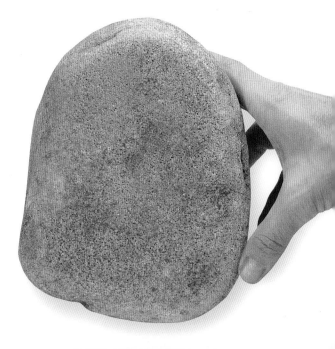

1 Layout

Once you've picked out and scrubbed your rock, use a pencil or marker to sketch the features. The head shape is a circle, fitting into the curving top of the rock between sloping shoulders. A half-round, widely spaced ear is set on either side. Ideally, the ears will fit neatly where the top of the head curves down so as to be at least partly visible. If they don't show at all from the front, lower the head circle slightly.

The muzzle is an oval with the lower end resting on the bottom line of the head circle and the top reaching the center of the circle. Place a round nose close to the end of the muzzle. Tuck eyes into place on either side of the muzzle's top. Bears have small, fairly close-set eyes, no more than one eye width apart.

Two front paws reach in from either side, curving down slightly. Draw a circular haunch just below each one, leaving open space between the two haunches. For the feet, draw two kidney-shaped soles that angle away from each other, then add the suggestion of toes.

There are few features on the back, other than the subtle indication of two shallow, **U**-shaped shoulder blades.

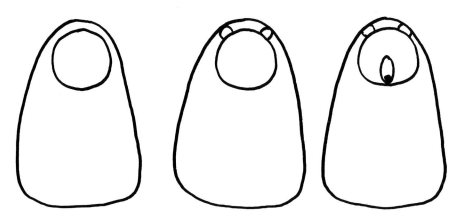

A bear's face can be broken down into easy-to-follow steps.

These step-by-step sketches will help you create a good layout every time.

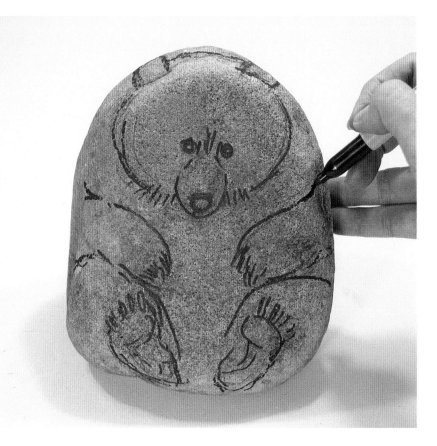

Begin with pencil, then go over your design with a marker. Once you've sketched in the guidelines, you're ready to paint.

Painting More Animals on Rocks

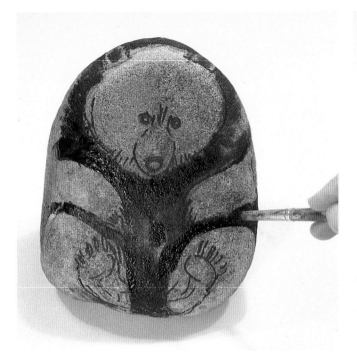

Outlining and shading with black paint sets off the main features.

Medium brown paint forms the base for this piece. Use it to cover every unpainted area of your rock except the soles of the feet.

2 Contours

Once you're satisfied with your sketched-in bear, use a medium-sized brush and black paint to begin creating the illusion of contours. Fill in the centers of the ears, then encircle the head shape with strokes that radiate out like short sun rays. Darken the outlines around the front legs and around the haunches, making the space between the haunches extra dark. If the shoulders look too high and prominent on either side (like a football player in padding), you can minimize their impact by painting them in a dark color, too. On the back side, lengthen a few strokes, carrying them down along the spine, then angling them out on either side to suggest the curve of shoulders.

Switch to brown paint and use it to cover just about every remaining area of your bear except the soles of the feet.

Paint around the sides. Note the amount of shading above and below the arm. Add more black to your piece if needed.

How to Paint a Bear

3 Details

An older brush with bristles that have separated is perfect for the next step, or you may use a liner brush. Mix enough white into a small amount of brown paint to get a pale tan shade. Start by outlining the ear circles, then fill in the sides of the muzzle and a narrow strip down the center to the nose. Next, work outward with a flicking motion of your brush to create a short fringe all the way around the head. Highlight the upper sides of the front legs and paws with shaggy strokes that angle down and inward. Do the same kind of highlighting along the curves of the two haunches, but keep the strokes vertical, pointing downward.

Add a touch of black to the tan paint to gray it down, and use this color for the soles of the feet.

Switch to a liner brush and black paint to outline the eye circles and fill in the nose leather. Next, outline the shape of the feet and add dark toes. Then go back around the lower portion of the muzzle to clearly define it.

A contrasting shade of tan simulates highlights along the tops of the arms and legs and around the face and ears.

Use a liner or detail brush to outline eyes, feet and toes with black, then fill in the nose.

These kidney-shaped feet are a whimsical touch. By adding a small amount of black to your tan paint, you'll have a shade for the soles that is slightly grayer than the fur highlights.

Painting More Animals on Rocks

This fur directional guide shows how you should slant your strokes for the most realistic look.

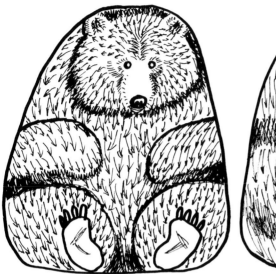
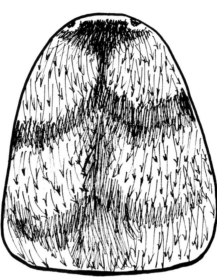
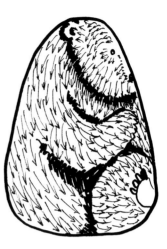

4 Fur

Taking the time to paint in lots of delicate fur lines will really make a difference in how well your bear turns out. With your liner brush, mix more tan paint and start adding layers and clusters of short fur lines around the lower half of the face. Sprinkle some longer lines into the chest area. When working on the top of your bear's head, you may find it helpful to turn the rock around for better control of your strokes. Encircle the eyes with very short pale lines, then work up from there as shown, leaving a dark "part" in the center of the forehead above the eyes.

Take your time with this step. These furry details give the bear its visual appeal, so pay close attention to their placement and density.

Turning your rock upside down may make painting these areas easier. Where you don't paint the fur lines is as important as where you do. Notice how blank spaces add visual interest.

Detail the back side with uniform layers of pale fur lines. The open space between groups of fur lines suggests contour. Leaving a curving space unlined below the shoulders will indicate the existence of shoulder blades.

To detail the back of your bear, turn it over and start just below the dark outline around the top of the head. Leave an unpainted strip along the spine, and make a fan-shaped cluster of strokes on each side. Begin with short lines, allowing them to get longer as they overlap and change angles. Don't paint over the darker shoulder blade curves. Just skip down and continue with more fur lines all the way to the bottom of the rock. Remember to detail the sides, too, and the upper portions of the front legs where they appear to be attached to the sides of the bear.

Once you've covered your bear with tan fur lines, mix some black paint into your Nutmeg Brown to get a deep brown color. Use it to add yet another layer of texture. Angle a series of short, dark lines along the center part, dividing the forehead fur to emphasize it.

Add a few darker strokes around the eyes just beyond the lighter strokes you did earlier. Make your strokes below the eyes quite dense to help the muzzle stand out. Add another layer of dark brown strokes to the chest right below

Darker lines emphasize some features and add depth to others. On the forehead, they call attention to the distinctive crease. Surrounding the muzzle with darker lines makes it seem to stand out from the rest of the face. Around the neck, dark brown blends with the lighter fur to give the head more dimension. On the back, use a row of darker lines to blend the shadows around the back of the head and to emphasize the shoulder blade contours.

the head for the same effect.

Now move to the feet and create lifelike creases to define the pad below the toes and the wrinkle beside the arch of the foot. Then tilt your rock back and add dark fur strokes to the bottom portions of the haunches. Turn the piece and make more dark lines along the lower edge of the back and sides.

The addition of two simple lines gives the feet more character.

These dark strokes around the bottom of the bear act like shading while adding texture. Remember to add them to the lower edges of the sides and back, too.

5 Finishing Touches

Mix up a tiny amount of light gray paint and use the tip of your liner brush to suggest a lighter top to the nose and two small nostrils, something like painting a lowercase **m** with the bottom lines curving in. Then use the same gray paint to dab in short marks that look like the bottoms of claws between the dark toes.

Clean your brush and touch the very tip in Nutmeg Brown. Paint a small half circle around the bottom half of each eye.

Touches of light gray contribute valuable definition to the nose and toes.

A half circle of brown paint warms up the eyes while leaving a dark center in place as an iris.

How to Paint a Bear

97

Clean your brush again and mix another small amount of pale tan. Use this color and the tip of your liner to create tiny prickles around the sides of your bear's muzzle, as well as a highlighting line following the curve just below the nose. Two bright dots of white give the eyes an intense sparkle.

In looking my bear over at this point, I decided that scattering some fur lines in a different shade of brown might improve the texture of the coat. I used Burnt Sienna, stroking it in randomly to blend with the rest of the fur.

The last touch was to add a highlight of pale tan to the tops of the bear's feet, just below the toes. I used my finger to smudge the wet paint, softening the effect.

Light paint and lots of prickly strokes add an outline of stubble to either side of the muzzle. Stroke in a curved line directly below the nose to connect the two sides.

Place white gleams in the eyes and suddenly your bear is staring right back at you!

Painting More Animals on Rocks

Smudge lighter colored highlights along the upper curve of the foot pad to suggest roundness.

A sprinkling of Burnt Sienna fur lines scattered throughout the coat enriches the texture.

A finished bear viewed from the front, side and back.

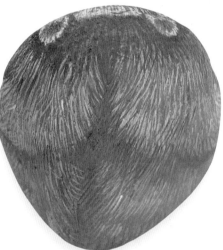

More Ideas . . .

Bears come in many colors, from polar bear white to honey brown to black, but the basic steps will remain the same. A panda, however, because of its markings, is handled a little differently.

A variety of finished bears.

HOW TO PAINT A PANDA

After laying out the basic bear design, divide the fur into the characteristic black and white pattern. Use gray to detail the black areas, and lighter gray with a touch of Yellow Ochre to detail the white areas.

Painting More Animals on Rocks

How to Paint a
Wild Cat

For sheer drama and beauty, it's hard to beat nature's wild cats: the leopard, lion, tiger and cheetah among them. Whether spotted, striped or maned, these graceful felines are exciting to look at and thrilling to paint. And while at first glance they may appear totally different, the same basic steps, with a few variations, will help you paint any of them.

In selecting suitable rocks, look for long, loaf-shaped or upright oval ones that have a flat bottom for stability and a high enough profile to do justice to these handsome animals. The rock can be as small as you wish, but I prefer one big enough to deliver real visual impact. Make sure the surface of your rock is clean before you start.

Here are three good examples of possible wild cat rocks. They all have broad, smooth sides and rather boxy oval or squared shapes in common.

See how simple sketches bring the animal out of these rocks?

1 Layout

Use a pencil to lightly sketch your animal's features. Begin by choosing the best site for the head. Ordinarily the narrower end, if there is one, seems to work best. If you're trying a lion you may want to use the wider end to accommodate a flowing mane. Once you've established which end to use, sketch a circle at the end that takes up 25 to 30 percent of the front surface of your rock. Check to see that the large, oval, upright ears will be visible when set far apart on top of your head circle. If not, erase the circle and lower it slightly.

Use a straightedge to divide the head circle into thirds. Then draw a second, smaller circle starting in the bottom third and extending out past it as shown.

Now place a triangular-shaped nose so that the one point rests against the bottom line of the head circle. Indent the top line of the nose at the center point. Divide the muzzle circle by extending a short line down from the nose that then separates into two lines, each one curving out to opposite edges of the muzzle.

Big cats have quite broad bridges above their noses, so draw two parallel lines upward, one from either point of the triangle top, ending them in the center of the head circle. Place two widely spaced eye circles on either side of the bridge lines. To give them their characteristic cat-like slant, extend a short line down from the inside edge of each eye, running close to and parallel with the bridge lines. Then sweep a line up and away from the outside upper edge of each eye. Below the muzzle area, make the chin line a bit more convex.

Next, move to the other end of the rock and sketch a round or oval haunch that is at least as big around as the head.

Putting together a leopard's head, piece by piece.

A few variations can transform a leopard into a tiger or lion.

If your rock is a lot wider at that end, make the haunch slightly bigger than the head. Then sweep a long, fairly thick but graceful tail in from the bottom of the rock around the haunch end. Give the tail a slight curve so that it points toward the face. If there's room beneath it, sketch in the suggestion of a rear foot. The front leg begins between the head and the haunch, about halfway down the side of the

rock. It should slant back toward the rear before crooking at the elbow. The foreleg extends to beneath the chin, with the paw showing at the end of the rock.

Sketching guidelines on the back side is easier since there is only a matching haunch circle and a rear foot, plus another folded front leg ending with a paw next to the first one.

To complete your basic layout, go

back to the sides of your main head circle and pare down the rounded sides there to give the sharpened appearance of feline cheekbones.

Lay out all big cats in the same general way. To make a tiger, draw the ears slightly smaller and add a fringed ruff that curves out from the cheekbone and back in at the bottom of the muzzle. For a lion, substitute the ruff for a much fuller mane that goes all the way around the head, with the ears standing out among the flowing tendrils. Once you are satisfied with your basic layout, go over your lines with marker to make them more distinct.

2 Contours

Now you're ready to begin painting. First, go over all your outlines with black paint and a medium-sized brush. Use solid black to fill in the space below the tail between the back toes and the bent front leg. Don't overlook painting in curved toe lines on the front paws even though they may barely show.

All the wild cats I've mentioned start with the same creamy base color. To mix it, squeeze out a large puddle of white paint and add just enough Yellow Ochre to turn it into a warm, very pale gold color. Use a large square brush to apply it to the entire surface of your cat, being careful to leave the black outlines of your layout uncovered. Remember to paint those paws hiding beneath the head, too.

Go over your guidelines with heavy black lines and fill in the area beneath the tail with solid black. On the back, simply paint in the curve of the haunch, the rear foot and the bent front leg.

Mix up a lot of this creamy white color so you won't run out. Try not to paint over the black lines; if you do, repaint them before going on.

Next, clean your brush and mix together a small amount of Burnt Sienna and Yellow Ochre. Start on the back side so you can practice blending this color into the contours, creating a softly shaded effect. Begin with the curving line of the haunch and work downward, scrubbing color into the area between the haunch and the front leg. Use your fingers to help blend the paint into the surface for a diffused look.

On the front side, again shade along the outside edge of the haunch, then darken the area directly above the tail. Scrub more paint along the outline of the head all the way around, smudging away from the head. Darken along the crease between the foreleg and chest. Then smudge in a line of shading along the bottom of the tail, blending it in so there are no harsh edges. Make a slanting mark that divides the lower portion of the haunch in half. On the face, blend the same color in soft half circles midway between the eye and the top of the muzzle to complete the undercoat.

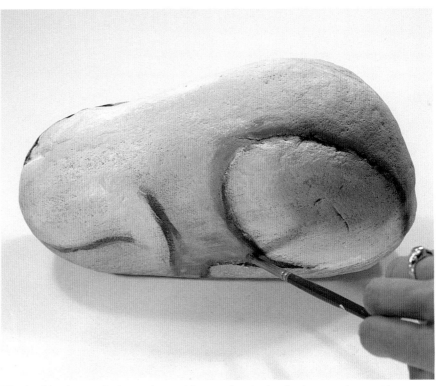

Blend golden brown shading in by scrubbing with a dry brush, then smudging with your fingers for a soft, diffused look. Starting on the back side will give you a chance to practice this technique.

Apply paint to the outside curve of the haunch and on the side above the tail, blending it out and away from these features. Around the head and the crook of the front leg again blend excess pigment out and away. Shade along the lower edge of the tail, the lower edge of the front leg and around the other side of the head. Lightly shade the base of the haunch and add a diagonal smudge to simulate the underlying muscle. Crescents of shading below the eyes complete this step.

Painting More Animals on Rocks

To fill in the nose triangle, mix red and white to get a deep pink, then add a touch of black to tone it down. Paint the nose, carrying the indent you made in the top line down through the center. Then fill in the ear centers with the same dusky pink.

Next, change to a smaller brush and white paint. Fill in the chin with white and outline around the eyes, leaving a border of black in place. Also outline the ears. Switch to black paint next and use a liner or other small brush to outline the eyes, nose and muzzle. Add a fringe of dark lines sprouting from the base of the ears and fanning into the centers. Now you should have all the bare rock surface painted with the exception of the eyes. At this point, the only differences between a leopard and a tiger are that a tiger has more reddish-gold patches on its face and bolder white markings around the eyes and along the beginnings of the ruff. The different black markings are where the two cats diverge completely.

Mix red and white to make a deep pink, then soften it with a touch of black and fill in the nose leather. Use the same color to fill in the ears.

Use white paint to color in the chin and touch up the inside edges of the muzzle. Outline around the eyes, then paint in clear, distinct ear outlines. Note how I left a narrow edge of black showing on either side of the ear lines.

Change to black paint and a liner brush and fill the bottom half of the ears with a tuft of black fur.

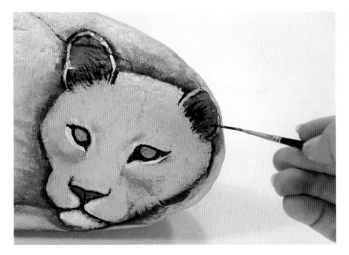

3 Markings

Select a short, tapering brush and use black paint to create your leopard's distinctive markings. Start just above one of the eyes and make a dark oval roughly as high as the diameter of the eye. Proceed to work up the forehead with a line of distinct, randomly sized dabs of paint, all smaller than the first, ending next to the ear at the top of the head. Do a matching line of dabs from above the other eye, ending by the other ear at the top of the head. Now imagine a wide **w** loosely constructed of small dabs of black paint and strung between the two first marks you made above the eyes. Add a small scattering of dots below these at the top of the nose bridge. Fill in the rest of the forehead with wandering rows of small, irregular dots. The dots can be larger and more oval in the areas under the ears, and should include ragged lines of connected dots along the base of the ears.

Make large black **V**-shaped markings that curve off from the outside corners of the eyes. These markings should be the same size as the first marks you made above the eyes. Also, make a connected line of markings under the lower white eye outlines. The rest of the face markings consist of small, irregular dabs along the cheeks and smaller, narrower lines along the tops of the muzzle, as well as neat rows of dark dabs following the curve of the lower muzzle where the whiskers will sprout.

Once the head spots are done, move to the front legs and make smaller irregularly shaped marks that gradually evolve as you move into the body area. The most important thing to remember is that your spots will look best if they seem random, so resist the urge to try and keep them uniform and tidy.

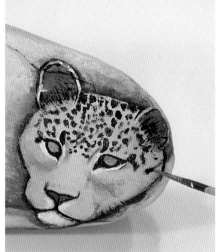

At the top is a detail of the head markings. A detail from the body markings is shown in the middle, and the tail markings appear at the bottom.

Begin your markings by balancing small oval shapes above the inside corner of each eye. Note how the subsequent markings vary in size and shape, yet follow a vague pattern of rows.

Duplicate these **V**-shaped markings at the outside corners of the eyes. Add rows of markings that form broken lines just below the two ears.

Painting More Animals on Rocks

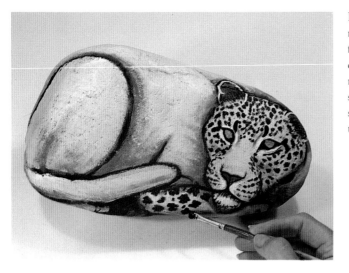

Begin the body markings with the front leg, where they consist mainly of irregularly shaped splotches with a few smaller dots scattered among them.

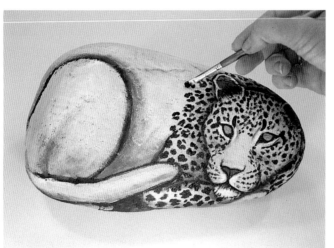

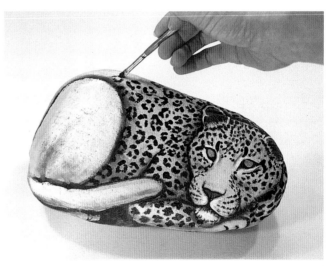

Do you see how the spot pattern slowly evolves into double sets of cupped spots and then into more defined circular shapes? Note also how each circular shape is different from those around it.

How to Paint a Wild Cat

Change shapes and direction, making some spots form nearly closed circles with empty centers and others disconnected in several places like broken bits of melting Lifesaver candies. The size of these markings should increase slightly as you paint your way from the front legs and neck toward the rear of the rock, but grow smaller again when you work down the tail toward the tip.

Handle the back side of your leopard in the same way. Note that there are occasional plain dots scattered among the other markings to add to the random look.

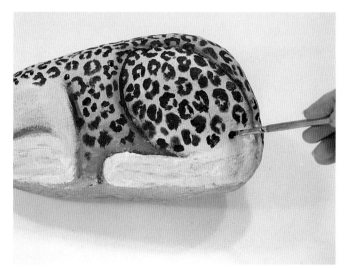

The markings at the base of the tail are similar to those on the haunch, but should get smaller and simpler as you work toward the tip.

This view shows how to handle the pattern of markings on the rear side.

When shown from the end, the way the markings flow together is evident. Notice how partial markings along the crease between the back and the haunch add to the illusion of curved contours.

Two curving black toe lines give the rear foot definition.

Painting More Animals on Rocks

When your spots have dried, use a small round or square brush to fill in the open centers of the markings with a mixture of Burnt Sienna and Yellow Ochre slightly more yellow than the mixture used earlier for shading. Dab this color into the middle of the markings all over the back and haunches of your animal until most of them are filled in.

4 Eyes

To paint the eyes, mix Yellow Ochre and white to get a medium gold color and carefully fill the eye circles, keeping them neat and round. Add more white to your brush to further lighten the gold, then stroke in a line of this lighter color along the outermost edge of the eye. When the eyes are dry, place black ovals in the centers, with the top of the iris touching the top of the eye circle. Next, blend a small amount of green paint with enough black to get a dark green color. Form a small half circle around the iris at the very top of each eye.

Fill in the centers of all your open markings with a mixture of Yellow Ochre and Burnt Sienna that's a shade more golden than the color used to shade the contours earlier.

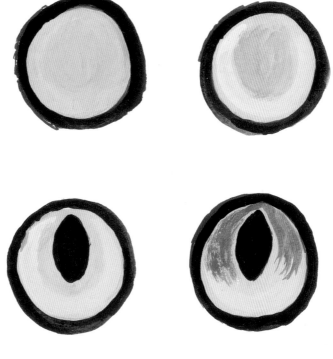

Creating a lifelike eye, step by step: (1) Fill in the entire eye circle with a blend of Yellow Ochre and white paint. (2) Add more white to this gold mixture and create a lighter ring around the inside edge. (3) When the eyes are dry, add black ovals that touch the top of the eye but not the bottom. (4) Mix green with a touch of black and shade the upper half of the eye.

5 Finishing Touches

Use your liner brush and white paint, thinned to a flowing but opaque consistency, to fill the leopard's ears with long, silky white fur lines. Then follow the line of the head, including along the top and around the curve of the muzzle, with a row of tiny white fur lines. Do more of these detailing strokes on the chin for definition.

If you'd like even more realism, add enough Yellow Ochre to your white to soften it to light cream, and use the tip of your liner brush to scatter white lines into the areas between the black markings on the face and along the body, particularly along the edges of main features like the top of the tail and around the legs. You can add as many of these texturing details as you'd like.

Long, curving white fur lines fill the ears.

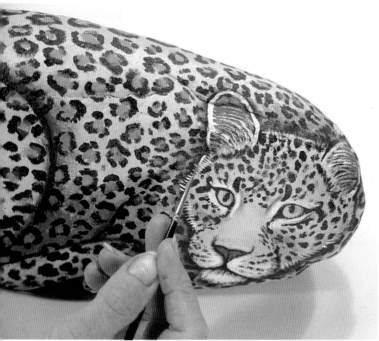

Go around the face with tiny, cream-colored fur lines to make the head stand out distinctly from the rest of the body.

Add a row of tiny lines to the top of the tail to set it off, and scatter them around the black markings to add attractive complexity to your animal's coat.

Painting More Animals on Rocks

To make the bridge of the nose seem to rise up from the face, paint along both sides with Burnt Sienna, smudging the paint with your finger or a damp brush to soften the lines.

In looking over the piece, I realized that the chest area directly below the outside edge of the head looked too plain, so I added some crisp white fur lines there among the markings. To finish my leopard, I mixed a scant brushful of water into my white paint to get a flowing consistency and added whiskers, then placed twin gleams near the tops of the eyes.

Dark lines of Burnt Sienna along the bridge of the nose will make it appear to stand out from the face. Soften the harsh edges with a damp brush or your fingertip.

A few last touches of white: clusters of crisp fur among the markings at the neck, long white whiskers arching gracefully from the muzzle, a few more eyelash lines to call attention to the eyes and white gleams, placed high in the eyes, to give the leopard its inscrutable look.

Two views of a finished leopard.

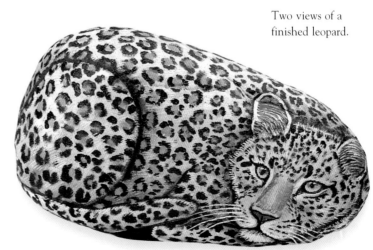

More Ideas . . .

While the basic steps to paint a tiger are the same as those for a leopard, there are slight variations in the shape of the head and the size of the ears. But it's the black markings that really set the two apart.

Finished versions of the rocks shown at the beginning of this demo.

HOW TO PAINT A TIGER

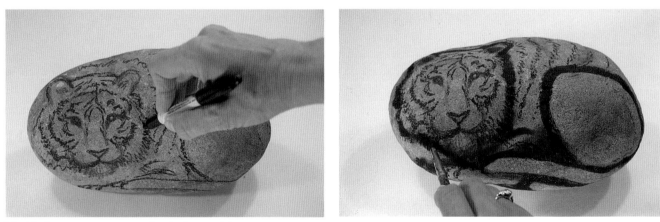

Use black to accentuate your sketched-in guidelines.

Apply a creamy base coat, leaving your outlines uncovered.

Painting More Animals on Rocks

Add Burnt Sienna shadows and shadings, blended into the undercoat.

Go over the facial features with black paint.

Dusky pink fills the ears and the nose triangle. Bold white markings add interest to the face.

Black markings and stripes unleash the tiger in this rock.

Side and rear views of the striped details.

Fill out the ruff with white fur lines.

Painting More Animals on Rocks

More details and highlights add to the realistic look. Eyes and whiskers complete this piece.

Another favorite feline subject is the elegant cheetah. I painted this one in profile. Save any good pictures you come across in magazines and other resources to help visualize how different poses might fit onto rocks.

Painting More Animals on Rocks

How to Paint a
Wolf

Over the years our perception of wolves has undergone a reversal. No longer the evil predators of legend, wolves now symbolize dignity and noble character in its natural state. Although there is nothing remarkable about the mottled coloring of the wolf's coat, the eyes—intense and brimming with intelligence—make this animal a favorite subject for painters.

The best wolf rocks are round or oval. You can paint a crouching pose on the vertical face of a rock that sits up; a curled pose works best on a flatter rock. If you choose the latter, look for a rock that is fairly thick in proportion to size.

Wolves come in colors that range from black to gray and tan, or even mostly white. The sandstone rocks available in my area are a brownish-beige color, and because I like to allow the natural color of the stone to show through, I'm going to paint a wolf in that mid-range hue. When your rock has been scrubbed and dried, you're ready to start.

Here are two good candidates for wolf rocks. A tall, narrow rock could become a "sitting up" wolf.

This round rock is suitable for a curled up pose.

The same rocks, with wolves sketched on, show how shape helps dictate layout.

Two basic layouts.

1 Layout

The rock I selected is basically round and about 4½″ (11.4cm) thick. It has one flat side but no flat edges, so the wolf will be curled up rather than crouching. As with most rock animals, an important factor in sketching the guidelines is determining the size and placement of the head. Since a wolf's head is quite broad, look your rock over and find the least curved, smoothest area.

Start by drawing an oval that takes up 25 to 33 percent of the surface of your rock. In placing this oval, keep in mind you will need room for two upright ears above it. If you set the oval too far back, the ears will disappear as the rock curves around.

The ears are large triangles set far apart along the top of the head. They will look more realistic if you extend the bottoms of the ear lines down a little into the head area.

Divide the head oval in half horizontally and center the eyes along that midline so they line up with the inside corners of the ears above. The eyes are simple circles, but a set of markings extending down from the inside corners, and a second set of horizontal markings from the outside upper edges, give them their intense expression. Note also that the eye circles themselves are not very big in proportion to the head. It's better to make them too small rather than too large.

You need to decide whether to draw your wolf's head raised so that the

1   2

3   4

Sketches 1 and 2 illustrate the importance of keeping the eyes small. Sketches 3 and 4 show the differences between a raised and a lowered head.

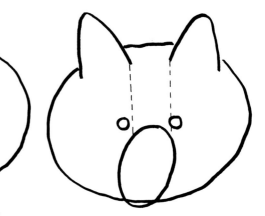

Breaking the layout of the facial features down into clear steps should make their proportions and relationships clearer.

Painting More Animals on Rocks

plump, oval muzzle appears slightly foreshortened, or to draw a more elongated muzzle that is pointing down. On a raised head, the bridge of the wolf's nose has a slight diagonal slant toward the center of the rock, and the end of the muzzle will be even with, or just slightly overlap, the oval shape of the head. On a lowered head, the muzzle is more pointed and will extend out past the shape of the head. As with all preliminary sketches, it may take more than one try to get all the elements of your layout right.

Leave enough room below and to the outside of the head to place two paws at the bottom edge. Divide the remaining surface of the rock between an oval haunch set lengthwise across from the head and a full fluffy tail sweeping in from the opposite corner of the rock to end just below the head. The space behind the head is for the shoulders and curving back.

Add a few fur marks to define the muzzle and the feathery ruff at the side of the face. When you are satisfied with the look of your layout, go over it with a marker to make your lines stand out.

2 Contours

Use a large, stiff brush and black paint to darken the contours, starting with the area between the head and the haunch, then moving to the top of the head behind the ears and along the outside edge of the face. Also outline around the front paws and around the tail. On the back side, solidly darken the lower portion of the rock near the bottom, then work down from behind the head to create several dark, curving sections. On the face, use a dry brush to paint a fan-shaped set of heavy strokes that start between the eyes and travel up and around them, tapering off before reaching the edges of the head. Similarly, paint fan strokes out from

the jowl area below each eye. For the haunch and tail, stroke in bold, rough lines with a dry brush as shown.

Next, use white paint and a smaller, stiff round or tapered brush to whiten the areas around the eyes and along the outside edges of the muzzle. Notice the

scattering of pale strokes across the bridge of the nose between the eyes. Make a series of dense strokes around the face to frame it, always working from inside to outside. Do a set of white strokes around and between the dark ones you made on the haunch and tail

After you've penciled in your wolf's features, go over your lines with a marker.

Use black paint and a stiff, dry brush to create the look of shadows, contours and contrasts so vital to this animal.

Select a smaller, but equally stiff, dry brush and white paint to highlight important facial features. The strokes have a softly diffused look, making them perfect underpainting for the detailed strokes to follow. Shading across the base of the muzzle between the eyes helps create the illusion that the nose is standing out from the rest of the face.

The white brushstrokes over the rest of the body are also applied with a dry brush. Leave the paint bold and thick in some places, and almost transparently thin in other areas, lending a random, haphazard look. It's okay to overlap a little, but for the most part, try to keep the white strokes separate from the darker ones.

earlier, with added emphasis along the top curve of the hip and the flowing upper portions of the tail. Since wolves tend to look a bit "scruffy," these strokes need not be perfectly orderly and neat. If you like the natural color of your rock, you may opt to allow some of that color to peek through.

Move on to the area behind the head. Use the same dry brush technique to create a series of soft, smudgy strokes that begin a short distance from the top of the head, leaving a defining edge of dark paint in place. The fur directional chart will help you visualize how these strokes contrast with the darker areas to give the suggestion of shoulders and other contours. Use a few very dry strokes to define the dark area between the head and haunch, again being careful to leave an outline of black in place around all the features.

3 Fur Details
Now change to a liner brush to create smaller white details, like the fuzzy prickles used to outline the ears. Narrow strokes also add texture and emphasis to the facial fur around the eyes and up into the forehead. You may also want to add finer strokes to the ruff areas along the side of the face. Place a line of short fur along the top of the head, too.

Turn your rock around and add a new layer of detail to the white fur you brushed in earlier. Since the fur along a wolf's neck tends to be longer, allow some of your strokes to flow out, overlap and even cross each other. The shoulder areas should be more highly detailed, while the subsequent sections down the back can be less so.

Rinse your brush and change to black paint to go over the same areas you just detailed in white, adding yet another layer of density and complexity to your wolf's coat. Here it is especially

Use this guide to help determine the direction of your brushstrokes for more realistic fur detail.

Use short, distinct rows of slanting strokes angling up along the outside edges of the ears, and a second, crisscrossing set edging upward along the inside edges.

Go over the white areas above the eyes with more fine lines. Use the fur directional guide to help determine how these detailing strokes should be applied.

These sparser strokes detail and define the forehead areas below either ear, leaving the center of the forehead dark.

Painting More Animals on Rocks

desirable to emphasize the previously painted darker areas, clustering dark strokes among them that then splay out into lighter areas. The idea is to interweave dark and light fur, while at the same time keeping some areas darker and allowing some areas to remain mostly white. A good example of this balance is along the top of the tail. You'll want to have enough white fur lines in place to help it stand out, but with plenty of dark fur lines to make it appear fluffy.

Add a row of short, dark lines just below the base of each ear, and scatter dark lines below the eye and throughout the ruff areas on both sides of the face. Outline the eye shapes with black, fill in the nose and go over the outlines of the muzzle with very short, prickly lines. Add some dry brushed lines to the outer side of the muzzle to soften the stark whiteness of it.

Look your entire animal over to see what other areas might benefit from additional dark fur lines. Some easily overlooked places are the front paws, the base and underside of the tail, and the back where it begins to curve with the shape of the rock.

Switch back to white and use your liner brush to highlight the tops and detail the centers of the paws. Add some white fur lines to the shadowy area between the paws and head, too.

Turn your rock around to add more layers of fur strokes to the white patches along the back, leaving the curving center line of the spine dark. Similarly, add a row of slanting white lines along the top of the tail.

Using black paint now, add depth and complexity to the dark spaces between and around your white strokes to really make them stand out. Start with the haunch, working from top to bottom, then do the same with the tail.

These rows of dark stubble just below the base of the ears add to the lifelike texture of your wolf. Note how the addition of a short, dense row of lines along the outside edges of the ears really makes them stand out.

4 Tint

Although I left some of the natural brown color of the rock showing through, I decided my wolf still looked too monochromatic. To fix this, I mixed up a watery combination of Burnt Sienna with a touch of Yellow Ochre, and applied it as a light wash to give some areas of the piece a warm brown tint. At this point you could tint with a straight gray shade instead, or gray with a tinge of Yellow Ochre.

As with all tints, your mixture should be light enough so that it doesn't alter the darker paint, yet not so watery that it simply rolls off the rock's surface. Making strokes on newspaper is a good way to test the color and strength of your tint. If it covers up the type, add water. Don't tint any white strokes around the edges of your main features; concentrate on areas like the center of the face, along the bridge of the nose and the fur spreading outward not quite to the edges of the ruff or the top of the head. Use tint to play up the half circles below the white outlines under the eyes. On the back use your tinting to emphasize the darker areas, again leaving the lighter edges plain. Add streaks of this warmer color to the center of the haunch and along the center of the tail.

Use your liner brush and black paint to outline the shape of the eyes, extending markings sideways from the upper outside corners. Emphasize the muzzle, too, by going around it with splinter-like strokes, then fill in the nose leather.

More important facial details include dry brush strokes across the outside half of the muzzle to create the look of shadow. Then create a row of strokes that begin along the outside edge of the muzzle and angle out in the direction of the markings at the corners of the eyes.

Even though they may not show much on your rock, don't neglect to add furry details to the front paws with white paint and your liner brush.

Use a wide brush and a carefully diluted combination of Burnt Sienna and Yellow Ochre to lightly tint the fur in the following areas: above and around the ears, in a random collection of streaks around the center of the haunch and down the center of the tail, along the bridge of the nose and the forehead, avoiding the outer edges. A light application of tint below the white markings under the eyes helps them stand out, too. Use the tint along the sides of the spine line, and among the patches of back fur.

Painting More Animals on Rocks

5 Finishing Touches

To fill in the eyes, mix a small amount of bright yellow with enough white to soften it to a buttery color. Use a liner or short detail brush and try to keep the yellow circles as neat and round as you can. Next, add a touch more white to the yellow paint on your brush, and add a half circle of this paler color to the lower outside edge of the eye. Rinse your brush. When the eyes are mostly dry, touch the tip of the brush first in yellow, then in black paint, and mix the two together to get a deep yellow-gray. Use this to create a second, smaller half circle inside the upper end of the eye. Let dry.

Now place small black ovals in the centers of the eyes, with the top of each oval just touching the top of the eye circle. A single pinpoint of white paint at the edge of these black irises will give your wolf a keenly intense gaze. Still using white, add a sprinkling of short fur to the wolf's chin. With a bit of black, soften your white paint to gray

Refer to the demo of the cat's eye on page 111 to paint in your wolf's eyes. Place a single dot of white paint in the same place on the edge of the iris in both eyes. It's vital that the dots be level and the same size to avoid a cross-eyed or cockeyed look.

I added a few tiny white lines to the chin to define it.

Gray touches on the nose give it new definition. Notice how the nostrils are simple **U**-shapes.

and create the look of a diffused gleam at the top of the nose leather, along with two small half circles below to indicate nostrils.

Use black paint and a steady hand to stroke in four or five arching whiskers on each side and dot in a few follicle marks near them.

Now look your wolf over carefully for any areas that may need touching up. At this point, I went over the gray nostril **U**'s with white to make them show up better and added long white fur lines to the inside of the ears. When you're satisfied, a light coat of polyurethane will protect the surface and bring out the rich tones in the paint.

Long black whiskers arching out from the muzzle, along with dotted rows of follicles, complete the black touches for this piece. Narrow white fur lines arch out from the inside edges of the ears. Reemphasize the half circles of the nostrils with white and your wolf is complete.

A collection of wolf rocks.

Painting More Animals on Rocks

Index